YOUR HORSE AND YOU

ALSO BY THE AUTHOR

A Horse in Your Life: A Guide for the New Owner

Your Horse and You

By HEATHER SMITH THOMAS

SOUTH BRUNSWICK AND NEW YORK: A. S. BARNES AND COMPANY
LONDON: THOMAS YOSELOFF LTD

© 1970 by A. S. Barnes and Co., Inc.
Library of Congress Catalogue Card Number: 70-107133

A. S. Barnes and Co., Inc.
Cranbury, New Jersey 08512

Thomas Yoseloff Ltd
108 New Bond Street
London W1Y OQX, England

ISBN 0-498-07473-0
Printed in the United States of America

To

Michael

who at an early age has a fondness for animals, and who was riding horses before he was born. He'll be riding them again as soon as his short little legs grow long enough to straddle fat Khamette, and it won't be many years before he's riding range with us.

CONTENTS

PREFACE

This is a book for anyone who is interested in horses, but it is especially for that person who owns a horse or who works with horses.

It is my hope that this book, the result of many years of experience (often of trial and error and discovering things the hard way) with our own horses, might help to answer some of the questions that the horseman might ask as he encounters problems or new situations in working with horses. In a sense this is a "do-it-yourself" book, built upon much of our "do-it-ourselves" experiences in raising and training and using horses on our isolated cattle ranch.

I want to thank several people who helped make this book possible. First, I'd like to thank Snowden Carter (editor) of the *Maryland Horse* magazine for letting me use portions of my articles which were published in 1967 and 1968. I'd also like to thank *The Cattleman* and *The Western Horseman* for letting me use parts of my articles that have appeared in these magazines. I'd also like to thank numerous horsemen who have helped me here and there along the way. I want to thank my husband, Lynn, whose patience and advice were much appreciated. Last, but not least, I thank our little son Michael, who "helped" in all phases of writing this book, giving me "time out" from the typing to feed, change, and "rescue" him from various predicaments as he learned to toddle around the house.

YOUR HORSE AND YOU

1

LET'S GET ACQUAINTED

Every horse owner must know a great deal about horses to properly use and care for them, as those of you who have had horses for any length of time have already discovered. Study, experience, and a mind open to new methods and ideas are the best teachers in the horse business.

My husband, Lynn, and I raise cattle but we have always raised a few horses, too. We enjoy our horses very much. They are a pleasure, but they are also indispensable to our ranching operation. We are ranching in the mountains near Salmon, Idaho, and raising Angus and Hereford cattle. We have a range operation, running our cattle in the surrounding mountains during summer months while we are putting up hay on the ranch.

During the months the cattle are on the range, one or both of us ride every day or two to check on them, moving some to better grass or water, making sure they stay in the proper fenced areas with the proper bulls, mending fence, keeping water troughs in good repair, packing salt to the cattle, checking on a late-calving cow, or bringing home any sick ones that need doctoring. Occasionally we get a case of pinkeye or foot rot, snakebite, and so on.

Besides the range riding, we use our horses during the branding and vaccinating each spring and fall. We also use the horses all year round checking through our cattle here on our strung-out creek-bottom ranch. Some of our rough terrain is easier to navigate horseback than by jeep; for checking cattle you just can't beat a horse—you can cover all the territory and check every cow, whereas a jeep is often limited to where it can safely go.

Thus our horses get a great deal of use. We estimate that on an average ride to check range cattle we ride ten to twenty miles (much of that in country almost straight up and down) and sometimes twice that

(l. to r.)
Lynn on Bambi and Heather on Khamette, checking through the cows and calves. (Photo by Clyde Stone, courtesy *Farm Profit* magazine)

far if we are checking *all* the cattle or moving them. Traveling this far every other day or so over rough country keeps a horse hard and in good working condition if he is properly cared for. Our horses deserve and get the best care we know how to give them because they are so vital to our ranching.

We have had a variety of horses through the years, but at present we have only five. I will introduce them to you briefly here because they will be mentioned throughout this book as examples. Nell is a seventeen-year-old brown mare (15/16ths Thoroughbred), used primarily by my younger sister when she comes to stay with us to help with the riding during the summer. Nell has raised three very nice foals in years past—two fillies for me and a colt for my sister Heidi.

Khamette is an eleven-year-old Half-Arabian bay mare that I raised out of a black grade Thoroughbred mare of Lynn's. Khamette has appeared as an "example" in many of my articles and was the subject for many of the photos that illustrated my first book, *A Horse in Your Life*. Khamette is a good ranch horse, an eager traveler, and enjoys working cattle.

Nikki is another Half-Arabian bay mare. She is out of Nell and is now an eight-year-old. She has more stamina and endurance than any

A view of the ranch in winter.

other horse we have. Bambi is an eight-year-old registered Quarter Horse bay mare that Lynn bought as a three-year-old. She's speedy at short distances, enjoys working cattle, but hasn't the endurance in the hills that our other horses have. And last but not least is Fahleen, Half-Arabian three-year-old filly, a full sister to Nikki. She and Nikki do not look much alike, however; Nikki favors their Arabian sire while Fahleen favors their chestnut Thoroughbred grandsire, in more ways than just color.

We usually ride Nikki and Bambi and use Khamette as an alternate. We're starting Fahleen under saddle and we will use her on short rides soon, too.

Since we use our horses for working cattle they must be agile and quick on their feet. We've found that the best way to train a horse for working cattle (teaching him to rein well, stop and turn quickly, follow a particular cow, etc.) is just to *use* him. A day's work on the range working cattle is worth more to his training than several sessions of schooling in an arena. He catches on more quickly and sees a purpose in what you are trying to teach him. And out of necessity he learns the proper balance and footwork needed in rough country. We've trained several excellent horses with no other "school ground" than their everyday work on the ranch.

Horses that are ridden as often and as hard as ours must be properly

Entering one of the ranch's dry-land pastures in the hills (author's brother on Khamette, dismounting to open gate).

Heather on Nikki and Lynn on Bambi, checking through cattle on the ranch in winter.

Refreshing our horses at one of the watering troughs for cattle on our range.

fed and conditioned for their work. They must be given good daily care, treated for any symptoms of lameness, and kept in excellent health. Lynn and I have had to learn many aspects of "doctoring" through experience, both with our cattle and with our horses. Since there are few veterinarians in our area we have been compelled to take care of most of our livestock problems by ourselves. We learn all we can from other ranchers and horsemen and from the vet when he is available. But there are times we have had to rely on our own judgment, using trial-and-error experiments.

We've learned that the average horseman *can* diagnose and treat a great many of the problems that arise, and we have discovered several methods of doctoring which have worked well for us. It is good to have the knowledge and supplies that you need for tackling the many minor problems that come up. Any horseman should be able to handle these problems in case a vet is not available. The value of knowing some practical do-it-yourself veterinary treatments cannot be overemphasized.

The conscientious horseman should know what problems he himself can take care of, and which ones are severe enough to require professional help. Knowing where to draw the line is important; you can save time and money if you don't need to summon a vet for something you can handle yourself, and you can save your horse's life or future usefulness if you know which problems you *can't* handle without professional assistance.

View of part of our range.

Some of our cows and calves watch us as we ride by.

Because we've raised several horses of our own, we've tried to learn as much as possible about the care of a brood mare before, during, and after foaling. We've learned to vaccinate against foalhood diseases and how to vaccinate all our horses each year for the diseases in our area. We've tried to learn all we can about raising and training horses (experience is the best teacher here, for each horse is different). We've learned how to treat wire cuts, puncture wounds, splints, rope burns, strains, proudflesh, and the many other problems that go along with living with horses. We shoe our own horses and therefore have had to learn how to prevent and correct abnormalities through proper trimming and shoeing.

Throughout our years of working with horses we've learned to cope with many of their ailments and problems, and we're still learning. As long as a person has horses he will be continually encountering new problems, and, I hope, learning what to do about them. I wouldn't wish problems on anyone, but I would hope that all horsemen have the desire to learn all they can about figuring out and treating the various problems that arise. We can care for our horses properly only if we are willing to learn.

It is my wish to share with you, in the chapters that follow, the various methods of treatment—and ideas in horse care and training—that we have used and found helpful in some of the problems encountered, and various valuable hints of horse management that we have picked up here and there along the way.

2

SOME FUNDAMENTALS
WORTH REVIEWING

The winter months find us indoors more often than out. We do some riding in winter, but for most of our horses wintertime is a vacation, and a well-earned one. We usually keep just two of the horses down at the ranch; the others winter out in a mountain pasture and enjoy a few months of freedom on hillsides covered with native grasses.

The winter months are good for catching up on the things we didn't get done earlier, like cleaning our horse equipment. In this chapter I'd like to mention a few things about taking care of tack and also give a few suggestions on using it properly. Much of this may be old hat to some of you, but if you are like us, it doesn't hurt to do a little reviewing on occasion and refresh your memory on some of these points.

It is good to make a habit of grooming your horse before every ride. Usually we try to have time to catch our horses, grain them a little and groom them before we saddle and bridle them. Sometimes we are in a hurry (if a cow is out, or the neighbor's cattle are coming down our lane or some other "emergency" arises) but still we brush the horse's back and withers before saddling, even if only with our hands, to be sure there is no dirt or other foreign material there.

Equally important is being sure there is no foreign material caught under the saddle blanket—dirt or twigs or wisps of hay. Often when we ride in heavy timber fir needles or twigs get under the saddle blanket and these must be removed or they will make a sore on the horse's back. Saddle sores caused by foreign matter pressed into the horse's back can be hard to clear up; continual riding will aggravate the open sore. About the only way to heal it is to stop riding the horse and use a soothing, heavy wound dressing that will keep the area soft as it heals. Saddle pads and blankets should be thick enough so as not to wrinkle under the

20

saddle; a wrinkle under the saddle can cause as severe a sore as a twig or burr.

Never slide the blanket forward. This goes against the lay of the hair. If your blanket or saddle slips too far back, take it off and resaddle rather than sliding it forward. When saddling, slide it *backward* into place. Sliding it forward ruffles the hair the wrong way and can make sores on the horse's back if he is saddled and ridden with the blanket in this position.

When using a western saddle, hook the right stirrup bow over the horn and lay the cinch across the saddle seat before you put the saddle on the horse. This will keep the stirrup bow or cinch ring from banging on the horse's side or elbow on his off side when you put the saddle on his back. Many horses have been made jumpy by their owner's carelessness. Most horses will learn to stand quietly for saddling if they are never hurt or spooked by a flopping saddle.

After you have put the saddle on his back, walk around to the off side and lower the cinch and stirrup, making sure everything on the rigging is lying smooth and straight. I have seen people cinch their horses with a twist in the latigo or with part of the stirrup leather or fender under the cinch because they did not check the rigging on the off side.

Return to the near side, hook the stirrup over the horn to keep it out of your way, and reach under the horse's belly for the cinch. Tighten it

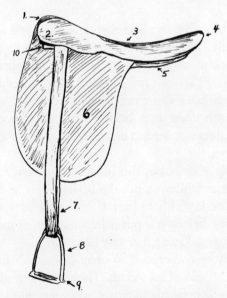

English Saddle: 1. Pommel, 2. Flap, 3. Seat, 4. Cantle, 5. Panel, 6. Skirt, 7. Stirrup leather, 8. Stirrup iron, 9. Tread of stirrup iron.

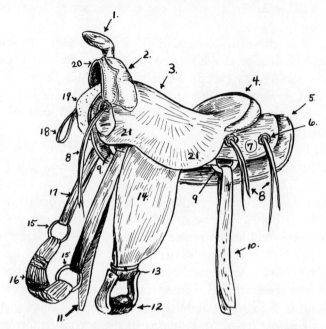

Western Stock Saddle: 1. Horn, 2. Fork, 3. Seat, 4. Cantle, 5. Skirt, 6. Rosette, 7. Back jockey, 8. Lace strings, 9. Dee rings, 10. Leather for flank girth for rear cinch, 11. Latigo, 12. Stirrup bow, 13. Stirrup leather, 14. Fender, 15. Cinch rings, 16. Cotton cinch, 17. Tug, 18. Rope strap, 19. Wool lining, 20. Pommel, 21. Front jockey and seat jockey.

enough to keep the saddle in place, then lead the horse a few steps before you cinch it snugly. This will settle the saddle into its proper place and you can then cinch it snugly without pinching the horse.

Cinch it slowly. Part of good horsemanship is keeping the horse as comfortable as possible. The cinch should never be so tight that you can't get your fingers under it. A horse with good withers and back holds a saddle well and does not need to be cinched as tightly as a low-withered, round-backed horse.

When bridling your horse, slip his halter off and refasten it around his neck to hold him while you put the bridle on. If he has no halter on, a rein around his neck will hold him. If it is a cold day, be sure to warm the bit in your hand before you put it into the horse's mouth; an ice-cold bit on a warm tongue doesn't feel very pleasant.

The horse can be encouraged to open his mouth for the bit if you slip a finger into the side of his mouth. There are no teeth there and even a stubborn horse will open his mouth if you press on the gum with your finger. Never clank the bit against his teeth. Ears are very sensitive, so

Saddling . . . cinch up slowly.

be careful with them. Rough handling of the ears will make the horse head-shy and hard to bridle. As you bridle your horse make sure all straps are straight and smooth and not twisted or they may cut into the horse and create a sore.

Be sure the bridle is properly adjusted. The bit should not be so snug that it pinches or pulls the corners of the horse's mouth and not so loose that it hangs in his mouth and bangs his teeth. An improperly adjusted bridle can rub sores in the corners of the horse's mouth. Like saddle sores, these are hard to heal if kept irritated.

Tack must be properly taken care of if we want it to stay in good condition. The saddle should be kept on a saddle rack or on a horizontal pole where it can hang straight. If a western saddle is kept on the ground or on the floor the skirts may curl or the stirrup fenders become bent and twisted.

Bridles, halters, and ropes should be hung straight when you put them away. You might want to wipe or wash the bit off after using it to keep it clean and sweet.

Blankets and pads should be brushed off and put where they can dry, laid over the saddle instead of under it. Rope halters will shrink if left out in the rain (one reason we never leave halters on our horses). Ropes should never be allowed to get wet.

Bridling . . . a finger in the corner of horse's mouth will induce him to open up for the bit.

Saddles, bridles, leather halters, and straps should be cleaned at least once or twice a year to keep them in good condition. With care, good equipment can last longer than your lifetime, but if neglected it can soon become useless. The mistake many people make is to use too much oil. This is just as bad as not using enough. Leather is kept in best condition by keeping it clean and pliable and not letting it stay damp over a long period of time. It should be kept in a dry place.

Proper care of the saddle begins before it is ever put on a horse. A new saddle should be oiled before it ever leaves the shop. Most saddle shops oil a new saddle because the wetting of the leather for fitting and tooling washes out some of the natural oil.

In cleaning a western saddle, the first step is the use of a vacuum cleaner. With a narrow nozzle, suck out the dust under the seat and jockeys, and clean the woolskin lining. After all loose dust is removed, work in a heavy lather, using saddle soap (either bar or paste) with a soft cloth. Remove the lather with a damp cloth and be sure there are no traces of soap left. When the leather becomes semi-dry you can dry-soap it with paste saddle soap.

In dry climates this paste can be left on as a leather dressing, but in wet climates use a regular leather dressing instead of saddle soap (dry soaping tends to draw moisture and keeps the leather too wet). Rough-out saddles can be cleaned with saddle soap but shouldn't be dry-soaped; use a good leather dressing instead.

In most climates a saddle should not require additional oil more than every three or four years, and even then do not oil too heavily. Too much

. . . fastening the throatlatch.

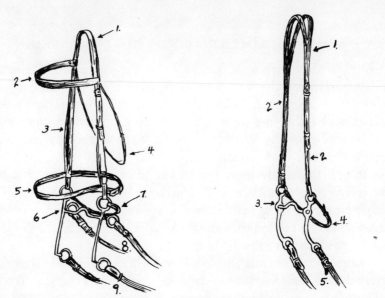

Double Bridle (left): 1. Crownpiece or headstall, 2. Brow band, 3. Cheek pieces, 4. Throat latch, 5. Nose band, 6. Pelham bit, 7. Curb strap, 8. Snaffle reins, 9. Curb reins.

Western Split-ear Bridle (right): 1. Crownpiece or headstall, 2. Cheek pieces, 3. Curb bit, 4. Curb strap, 5. Reins.

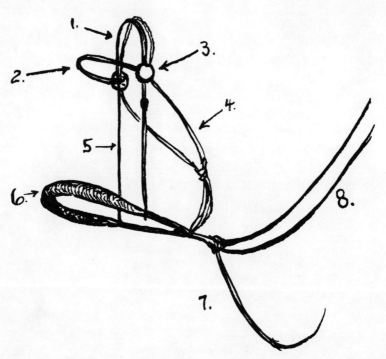

Hackamore: 1. Crownpiece or headstall, 2. Brow band, 3. Rosette, 4. Throatlatch, 5. Cheek piece, 6. Nose band, 7. Lead rope, 8. Reins.

oil is as harmful as not enough, for it rots the leather. In damp climates it also causes the leather to absorb too much moisture.

Don't oil a saddle in very hot weather. Neat's-foot oil, made of animal fats, is a good natural oil for leather, but a good grade of vegetable oil can also be used. Never use oil with a mineral base; it will burn the leather.

Saddles kept in a damp place will draw moisture and can develop mildew that is hard to get rid of. To get rid of white mildew spots, wash the tack thoroughly with saddle soap, sponge it with a strong acid vinegar, and put it out in bright sunlight for several hours. Then go over it with leather dressing.

Tack actually stays in best shape if it is used often. Using it keeps it out in the air and sunshine and the motion of the horse keeps the leather flexible.

If your saddle must be stored for a long time it should be moved periodically so that the leather doesn't remain in one position and get stiff. And remember to mothproof the wool lining.

One last suggestion: Take your saddle to your local saddle shop every three or four years to have it checked for defective parts, or take it apart yourself and check it. This could save you a serious accident.

Happy saddle cleaning!

3

FEEDING HORSES

A horse inherits certain potentials for growth and for speed, strength, and endurance, but how well these potentials are developed depends much upon the feed the horse eats—whether it is adequate in quantity and quality. A horse with good breeding may still develop poorly and perform poorly on insufficient or improper feed. Horses must be fed properly in order to have a long life of usefulness. They should not carry excess weight or their health will be impaired and they won't be able to perform as they should.

Let's look at some of the factors involved in feeding a horse. If your horse is kept in a pasture, the pasture should be large enough to grow the grass needed to support him. The size of the pasture which will support your horse depends on the types of grasses in it, the fertility of the soil, and the amount of moisture it gets. It will take more dry-land area to support a horse than good irrigated pasture, but some of the native dry-land grasses are the best horse feed. Irrigated pasture grasses sometimes have too high a moisture content; horses get their fill before they've eaten enough to provide them with the proper nutrients. There is more food value in the dry-land grasses by volume. The ideal horse pasture should cover at least two or three acres per horse and should contain some good types of palatable grasses.

Our ranch horses are kept on irrigated pasture in the summer and fed grain when we are using them regularly. They are kept on dry-land range in the winter and stay in excellent condition with no additional feeding, during a normal winter. Our dry-land pastures have several varieties of grass which horses thrive on. Some of these are western blue-bunch wheat-grass (Agropyron spicatum), which is our best range grass and very palatable and nutritious at all stages of growth; Sandberg bluegrass (Poa secunda Presl), a native grass not nearly so tall as blue-

Comparing the Digestive Tracts of the Horse and the Cow
(not drawn to scale)

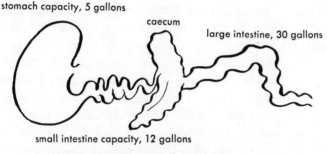

stomach capacity, 5 gallons

caecum

large intestine, 30 gallons

small intestine capacity, 12 gallons

Digestive Tract of the Horse

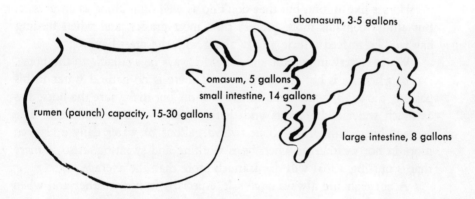

abomasum, 3-5 gallons

omasum, 5 gallons

small intestine, 14 gallons

rumen (paunch) capacity, 15-30 gallons

large intestine, 8 gallons

Digestive Tract of the Cow

(Photo from the author's feeding article in the April 1968 issue of *The Maryland Horse*)

bunch wheatgrass, but which horses like; and Idaho fescue (Festuca idahoensis), a short grass that horses and elk are very fond of, and which dries well and makes good winter feed. Winter snows soften up these native grasses and make them more palatable.

The horse is a roughage consumer by nature, but this fact has been overemphasized so much that he is often expected to eat grass or hay of poor quality. The horse is actually less efficient in his digestion of roughages than a cow or a sheep. This is because digestion takes place faster in the horse (he does not chew his cud and "reprocess" his food); the

feed passes through his system more quickly than through that of rumi-
nants, and some types of feed are less fully utilized.

The greatest single factor in determining the quality of pasture
grasses and hay is its stage of maturity. The older and drier the grass, the
less palatable it is. Mature grasses are coarse and are not as digestible as
green and growing ones. Some of the hay grasses, timothy, smooth
brome, intermediate wheatgrass, and others, are good horse feed if grown
in fertile soils and grazed while young. Any of the pasture grasses or
dry-land grasses are preferable to swamp grass (which is very coarse).
Pastures should always have adequate drainage to avoid swampy soil.

Mature hay has very little nutritive value, whereas hay that is har-
vested while young (still in the flowering stage, not yet gone to seed)
is highly digestible. A horse can more fully utilize the easily digestible
young feeds, and is also able to eat a larger quantity, due to the faster
rate of digestion.

Horses like alfalfa, but they don't do as well on it alone as on grasses.
But alfalfa contains more protein than most grasses, and when feeding
hay we like to feed a little alfalfa along with the grass hay.

Water is very important and should always be available to the horse,
except when he is hot from exertion. If there is no natural water in his
pasture, a trough, water tank, or tub will do, but make sure the horse has
as much water as he wants and that it is always clean and fresh. The
average horse will drink about twelve gallons of water daily and even
more in hot weather or when he is working and sweating. Also, a mare
that is nursing a foal will drink much more than the average horse.

A horse should always have salt, especially in hot weather and when
he is working hard. It helps to combat fatigue by replacing the salt that
the horse sweats out of his body.

Iodized salt should be fed in parts of the country that are lacking in
iodine. You can find out from your vet whether your area is deficient or
not. Mineralized salt has minerals added. Under good conditions of pro-
duction the normal horse will get the minerals he needs in a good diet
of grasses and grains. But where feed is grown in deficient or depleted
soils, the horse will need these additional minerals.

Salt comes in many forms. Our horses seem to prefer the block type
to the granulated type; they like to lick and chew on the blocks. A horse
will not eat too much salt. He eats only the amount his body requires, so
salt can and should be kept available to him at all times.

If rainfall is frequent or if there is no high spot in your horse's pasture
that is free from irrigating water, you will have to take the necessary
precautions to keep the salt dry, making some kind of container and cover
for it. I can remember my dismay when, one time in my youth, I put a

Inexpensive Feed and Watering Devices (from top to bottom): bucket holder made from an old tire; container for salt, minerals, or grain that can't be tipped over easily—made with four boards and a bottom; feed bunk made from an old tractor tire; water tub made from half an oil barrel—with pipe welded around the top to cover the sharp edge.

block of salt in the pasture for our horses, only to find it half-dissolved the next day when my father irrigated the pasture.

If a horse is on pasture he may or may not need additional feeding, depending on the quality of the pasture, the needs of the individual horse, and how much he is being used. Pregnancy increases the feed requirements of a mare, but increases it significantly only during the last quarter of her gestation period. Many horse owners seem to think that a mare must be fed extra as soon as she becomes pregnant. As a result mares are often overfed and are too fat at foaling time. A mare's real need for extra feed is during that last quarter of her pregnancy and after she foals and is producing milk. The average 1,000-pound mare produces between 5 and 6 gallons of milk per day. A lactating mare will need two to three times as much feed as she would require for body maintenance alone.

Feed requirements of individual horses vary, but in general a horse doing light work (2 to 3 hours daily) requires about 50 percent more energy than one doing no work. A horse doing medium work (4-5 hours daily) uses 70 percent more than one not working. And one doing heavy work requires even more feed. But these are general figures; they'll vary according to the type and volume of the work, the condition of the horse, the time of year, and so on. Horses need more feed in winter than in summer.

The U.S. Cavalry had a good general rule for feed, for horses doing steady work. Horses were fed one pound of grain and 1.1 pounds of hay for every 100 pounds of body weight. On days when the horses were not ridden, grain feeding was cut down considerably.

If you are using a horse regularly, feed him grain. A horse that is an easy keeper may stay in good condition on pasture alone even when ridden a great deal, but he will have more energy and endurance if fed grain. Our Half-Arabian mare Khamette stays fat on pasture alone and even on rather poor-quality feeds. An owner of a horse that is such a good keeper is tempted to use him without feeding him extra. But we have found that Khamette goes much farther in a day if fed grain. We get the best performance from this mare when she is kept off pasture on a limited amount of hay (to keep her from being too fat) and a fair portion of grain to give her the needed energy for strenuous rides.

With the average horse, the harder he is worked, the more feed he needs, and he can handle the extra feed better in concentrate than in bulk form.

No two horses are alike. You will have to discover the amount of feed that seems right for each. Some are gluttons, others are nervous and picky eaters. Some horses eat slowly, others eat too fast. Some need more feed than others. Some need more hay, others more concentrate. To illustrate a few individual differences: Khamette and Bambi will eat hay that Nell won't touch. Bambi, Nell, and Khamette all bolt their grain, while Nikki takes forever to eat hers. When Fahleen was a weanling and yearling she played with her grain; I had to spread it over the entire bottom of the feed trough to keep her from wasting it, for if it was in a

Our young horses are fed grain in addition to pasture or hay. (Fahleen as a weanling)

pile she nosed it and flipped it around, tossing some on the ground.

Rations should always be changed gradually, and regularity of feeding is important. Abrupt changes can cause digestive disturbances. Small amounts given regularly are better than a huge amount given at once. This is especially true of grain. Too much grain can founder a horse. And, remember the horse's small stomach capacity—his system can utilize only a certain amount at a time. The rest passes on as waste.

When feeding grain it is best to split it into two portions and feed twice daily. Horses that are being fed a large ration of concentrates (horses doing strenuous work, mares nursing foals, young stock, etc.) can be fed three times a day, so that none of the separate feeding portions is very large. Grain should be cleaned up within thirty minutes, and usually in less time. If a horse doesn't clean up his feed within thirty minutes, the amount should be reduced.

Never overfeed a horse. A horse that is too fat cannot perform well and will tire easily. If he has a crammed stomach from eating too much, he will not feel like working. Excessive fatness in brood mares and stallions interferes with fertility. Overly heavy horses are more prone to founder, especially "road founder" caused by concussion when they are ridden hard. Too much feed, especially when a horse is not working, can produce serious metabolic disorders, such as azoturia. In azoturia,

Mare and foal on pasture: Scrappy and two-month-old Khamette.

large stores of glycogen have been laid down in muscles during a period of idleness on full rations, and when the horse exercises, this glycogen is rapidly metabolized to lactic acid. If lactic acid is produced faster than it can be removed in the blood stream, accumulation occurs, causing hard painful swelling of the large muscles. Symptoms develop about fifteen minutes to one hour after the beginning of exercise. The horse sweats, becomes stiff, and is reluctant to move. Symptoms may disappear in a few hours if the horse is given complete rest immediately, but in severe cases the horse may die. To prevent such disorders, cut down the horse's grain ration considerably on days he is not ridden or exercised.

Don't overfeed young growing horses. Bones, tendons, ligaments, and joints are more easily injured when the horse is carrying excess weight, especially when these tissues are still immature and growing.

Foals and young horses fed too much grain or too many vitamins and minerals may have their body chemistry upset by this imbalance. Some nutritional diseases are caused by *too much* supplementation of vitamins and minerals, and too much grain can interfere with the proper absorption of calcium, causing soft bones. Soft bones and excessive weight can cause permanent damage to the growing horse. Calcium deficiency in these young horses cannot be corrected by feeding calcium; they cannot absorb the calcium that is already passing through their systems unless their grain ration is drastically reduced.

Some horsemen today (especially in the stock horse breeds) try to push their foals and young horses to fast growth and extra pounds. This is not natural or healthy. The horse is not a beef animal! Many people today are in too big a hurry. A good horseman has *time* to let a foal grow up and mature properly before he starts to ride it.

On our ranch our young horses have always been fed grain, but the main item of their diet has been natural feeds, preferably the dry-land grasses when possible, and the best hay and pasture available when they are being kept up. When we stop to consider the fact that thousands of good horses have been raised in the past on nothing but natural feeds and the grains available, we are not so apt to rush out and buy the newest brand of special feed for young horses which the advertising claims will speed them to better and faster growth. Please don't misunderstand me. Young stock should always be fed properly and well, but feeding can be, and often is, overdone.

If a horse lacks appetite or takes a great deal of time to eat his food, he may have teeth problems and you ought to have your vet check him. If a horse eats large quantities of feed but does not stay in good flesh or has a poor coat, he very likely has a heavy infestation of worms. Consult your vet about internal parasites, find out what kind the horse has and how to treat them. It would be wise to have all your other horses wormed, too. Consult your vet for a good yearly worming program.

Never give a horse spoiled or moldy feed. Moldy hay is especially dangerous and should never be fed. It can fatally poison a horse and can cause pregnant mares to abort. Horses can get respiratory ailments from dusty or moldy hay. Discard all moldy hay. If your hay is dusty, you can shake it to remove some of the dust, then sprinkle it with water to settle the rest. Extremely dry hay is usually dusty. It doesn't hurt the horse to *eat* dusty hay (except that dry hay is usually less palatable than properly cured hay)—the damage is done by his breathing the tiny hay particles into his lungs. These cause irritation and can lead to infection. The result is a cough and a runny nose, or even worse—heaves or pneumonia. Some horses are more susceptible to respiratory problems than others.

If well cured (dry—not damp and moldy—but not *too* dry or it will be sun-bleached and have lost much of its vitamins and feed value) both grass and legume hay make good horse feed. Grass hay is less likely to be dusty or moldy than alfalfa and other legume hay. The main problem with legume hay is that horses like it and will eat too much. Grass hay can be fed more freely, but legume hay should always be fed sparingly to avoid possible digestive upsets.

There are several ways to feed hay. Overhead racks are handy if the hay is dropped down from a loft above, but it is unnatural for a horse to reach *up* for his food, and dust and chaff often fall into his eyes. Mangers and feed bunks are a good way to feed hay if they are low. They allow the horse to reach down; he needs to exercise his neck muscles as though he were grazing. The only disadvantage with mangers and bunks is that they need to be cleaned out periodically. There are several disadvantages to feeding on the floor of a stall or on the ground. The horse may pick up worm eggs from manure and become infested with internal parasites. He also scatters some of the hay and wastes it. Hay that has been urinated on is never eaten and is no good even for bedding. When feeding on ground that is sandy or gravelly, the horse may swallow sand when picking up the last wisps of hay or leaves of alfalfa. If this continues over a period of time, the sand can accumulate in the caecum and cause impaction.

If you live in an urban area you may have wondered about the possibilities of using lawn clippings as horse feed. Grass clippings do make good feed, especially when dried. Because lawn grass is young and growing it is highly digestible and nutritious. But be cautious when first starting a horse on this kind of feed; don't feed too much at once. Because of its palatability, horses will overeat and get digestive disorders. The best way to start a horse on grass clippings is to replace only about a fourth of his hay with a similar amount of clippings, then gradually increase the clippings until the hay has been entirely replaced.

Freshly cut clippings are 70–80 percent water and the horse will need supplementary feed because he can't eat enough volume of clippings to provide for his needs. Fresh clippings tend to give the horse loose bowels because of their high water content. If you do feed fresh clippings be sure they are not piled for any length of time, especially in hot weather, or they will spoil and mold. Clippings that are allowed to dry before being gathered are much better.

Perhaps you have wondered about pelleted feeds. Pellets are not new in the livestock industry—we've been feeding them to our cattle for many years—but they have only recently been favored by horse owners. Many feed companies are now offering pelleted feeds for horses.

Pelleted feeds are just ordinary horse feeds ground up and processed and compressed into pellets. Some pellet feeds are made from various grains. Others contain nothing but hay. Still others (called a "complete" pellet) contain hay plus grain. Most of these pelleted feeds have vitamins and minerals added. We have never used the "complete" pellets on our ranch because we have hay and pasture readily available. Pelleted concentrates (grains) are handy and we have used them on occasion; pellets can be fed in some instances where grain cannot, as on the ground or snow to horses on winter pasture, and we have also used them on hunting trips and pack trips in the mountains.

The controversy in the horse world over pellets is not over the pelleted concentrates but over the pellets that are a complete ration in themselves—the ones that are designed to be the *only* source of food for the horse. These pellets have advantages and disadvantages.

Here are some of the advantages of the complete pelleted feed. Rations can be easily measured for each horse. Contents are uniform. Pellets are convenient, easy to store or to transport, taking up very little room compared to the usual grain and cumbersome bales of hay. They can be carried on a trail ride or pack trip or to a horse show. There is no waste; when fed in a manger or tub, every bit is eaten. The ingredients are nearly all utilized by the horse and very little passes on as manure, making less clean-up problem in stables (on an ordinary diet some of the hay and grain passes through the horse undigested).

A horse fed nothing but pellets has a trim belly, never a "hay belly." Older horses and horses with bad teeth seem to do well on pellets. Horses are less apt to founder on pellets when they eat too much. There is practically no dust; and if kept dry, pellets don't get moldy. Horses with heaves often do better on pellets than on hay.

But there are disadvantages as well. I have seen pellets that crumbled too readily. Sometimes when a horse eats too fast he may get some of the crumbled particles in his windpipe and inhale them, causing irritation and coughing. The main disadvantage to feeding a complete pellet ration is that many horses will chew wood.

Many horsemen argue against pellets by pointing out that nature equipped the horse with a digestive system for handling roughage in its natural form. Their theory about why pellet-fed horses chew wood is that these horses crave roughage. Pellets are made of roughage, but it is all ground very fine. The horse may not feel full and thus resorts to chewing wood. Some nutritionists feel that a horse normally requires a moderate "fill" of roughage to satisfy his normal body functions. The bulk fibre of roughage has practically no nutritional value in itself, but the horse requires a moderate proportion of it to stimulate the digestive processes. These nutritionists feel that roughage therefore assists in the digestion and assimilation of the digestible matter the horse eats.

Other nutritionists have done experiments trying to show that horses can be kept in good physical condition on a balanced concentrated ration without roughage. The theory behind these experiments is that horses do not need roughage, but nutrients.

Another theory about the wood chewing is that the horse is bored. Pellets are eaten much more quickly than hay and grain and the horse has more time to be bored and so chews more wood. But my own feeling in the matter leans toward the roughage-craving theory. Perhaps the complete pelleted feed for horses might be somewhat comparable to humans taking meals in a series of pills or cubes that contain all our nutrient requirements. Even though our requirements would be satisfied, our stomachs would tell us we were still hungry and we would want to nibble on something. Many horses chew wood badly when first started on pellets, then taper off after they become adjusted to the new ration and their stomachs have shrunk somewhat.

Another factor to be considered in the pellet controversy is that hay used in making pellets must be of the highest quality. If you have ever bought hay for your horse, you know that there are sometimes bad bales or bad spots in a few bales among even the best loads of hay. How much sorting of hay goes on at the commercial mill that puts out the pellets? This deserves some inquiry.

Another possible disadvantage in pellets is that if a horse accustomed to a diet of pellets accidentally gets into a pasture or finds access to grass or hay, he may be in danger of colic or impaction because his stomach and intestines have shrunk and he cannot manage the extra bulk.

Pellets are expensive if you can get good hay and pasture that is cheap or home-grown. But if you are buying all of your horse's feed anyway—hay, grain, and supplements—pellets are practical. This is why more and more owners of pleasure horses will probably use pellets; and as scientists and feed manufacturers learn more about proper horse nutrition, the pellets will undoubtedly be improved still further. Pelleted feeds cost anywhere from $40 to $100 a ton, depending on the brand and upon your locality. That seems expensive until you think of the small amount you have to feed, the lack of waste, the fact you don't have to buy other feeds, and so forth. The controversy over proper roughage goes on, but pelleted feeds are here to stay, and you may very well discover that they are practical and convenient in your locality and individual circumstances.

4

GIVING "SHOTS" AND VACCINATIONS

The old saying that an ounce of prevention is worth a pound of cure applies very well to horses. Most people who own horses have some sort of yearly vaccination program; a great deal of trouble can be avoided by inoculating our horses against contagious diseases.

Our horses are vital to our ranching operation and we can't afford to let them be sick. Treating a sick horse can be time-consuming and costly, plus the fact that the horse might be useless to us for several months during the time we need him most. Leaving a horse unprotected from disease is not worth the chance of having him suffer or even die.

Which diseases you vaccinate for depends on where you live. Some diseases occur in nearly all areas (tetanus and sleeping sickness, for instance); others appear only in certain localities. Sleeping sickness (equine encephalomyelitis) and tetanus are both very serious diseases with a high mortality rate. These should be on your list of yearly inoculations if there is any chance at all that your horse might encounter them.

Here in eastern Idaho we have always vaccinated our horses against sleeping sickness. We are fortunate to live in an area where tetanus is not a danger. But in recent years other diseases have come into this region and we've added vaccinations against strangles and influenza to our list. Ask your vet for advice on prevalent diseases in your area.

Sleeping sickness (also called "brain fever") is caused by a virus spread by mosquitoes. In the United States there are two types of virus. In years past we needed to vaccinate only for the western type, but now with the greater spreading of diseases around and across the country, we must use a different vaccine which immunizes against both types. In our area the disease is most likely to occur in the hot month of August, so we vaccinate in May or June before the flies and mosquitoes are out in force.

39

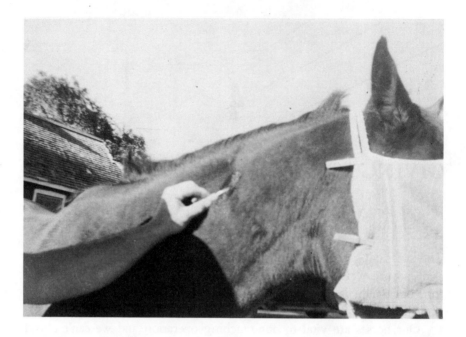

Giving a sleeping-sickness shot. The shot is administered with a very small needle—between the layers of the skin on the horse's neck. The vaccine must be injected slowly and create a "bubble" about the size of a marble.

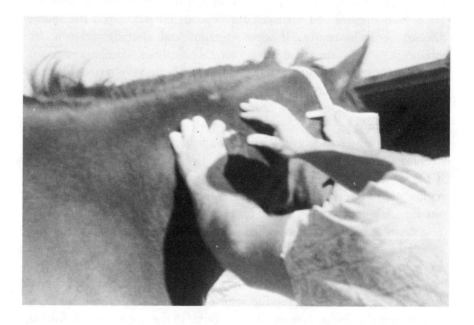

Sleeping sickness attacks the horse's brain and spinal cord and in many cases death results. First symptoms are fever, dullness, and sleepiness. Then the horse loses coordination of his muscles, staggers and falls. The disease can occur at any age, to either sex. There is no real cure. The only thing that can be done is to vaccinate *before* the horse gets it.

Sleeping sickness epidemics are becoming quite rare because most horsemen vaccinate against it. However, there has been an upswing in number of cases in recent years because some people, thinking this disease a thing of the past, no longer bothered to vaccinate. One of our neighbors lost a horse a couple years ago for this reason. Vaccinating every year is certainly worth the trouble if you can avoid the heartache of losing a good horse, or seeing one become permanently disabled, as my father did on the farm where he grew up—in the days before vaccine.

Sleeping-sickness vaccine is given in two doses (one cc. each) seven to fourteen days apart. A sleeping-sickness shot is somewhat difficult to give, for it must go between the layers of skin on the horse's neck. A very tiny needle is used. Because the needle is so small and the vaccine must spread apart the layers of skin, it goes in rather slowly, and the horse must stand absolutely still.

The principle of giving this shot between the skin layers is to create a "bubble" of vaccine which will absorb *slowly* into the horse's system, usually taking several days or even a week. A horse can have a severe reaction to the vaccine if it is absorbed too rapidly, as would happen if it were injected into a muscle. Horses have been killed by injection of this vaccine directly into a vein. If the vaccine makes a visible bubble in the skin (about the size of a marble) it is in the right place and will be absorbed slowly. There is no danger when the shot is given correctly, and it's not hard to do correctly when you know how. But I would not advise the beginner to try it without a lesson or two from a vet or from some other person who has had experience.

Some horses get a mild reaction to these shots. We have one mare, Khamette, whose neck swells where the shot is given (the bubble spreads out as large as a pancake) and she does not feel quite up to par for a day or two. It is wise not to ride a horse for a day or two after vaccinating for sleeping sickness, especially if a reaction to the shot is evident.

Sleeping sickness may be almost a thing of the past, thanks to vaccine, but today it seems that there are more diseases around than ever before. This is because horses do a lot more traveling—to horse shows, rodeos, and trail rides all over the country, and horses are often sent clear across the country to be bred. In this day of trailers and vans and jet-age horse transportation, there are many opportunities for diseases to spread. Vaccinating for the most prevalent diseases is now a must, especially if you ride with other horsemen, keep your horse at a stable where he might come in contact with other horses, or if you plan to show your horse.

I had planned to show our weanling Half-Arabian filly, Fahleen, several years ago at our local fair, but stayed home because there was a minor epidemic of influenza running through the horses in and around town. When it comes to communicable diseases, we are glad we're somewhat isolated here on our ranch, thirteen miles from town and up a creek. But one is no longer completely isolated, and to take the chance of not vaccinating your horses because you are isolated is just that— taking a chance. So that year, for the first time, we vaccinated against influenza.

It was a particularly bad year for influenza in our part of the country, because it was such a good year for flies. We had a real bumper crop of little face flies, the kind that spread pinkeye in cattle. These insects help to spread influenza in horses. When a disease is spread by insects rather than by direct contact (horse to horse) we can never really be isolated. How far does a fly or a mosquito travel? It's hard to say, but I know that they will often follow an animal for several miles, and can easily come into our "isolated" area by following a cow or a horseman traveling from an infected area.

Besides spreading disease, the face flies are bothersome to the horses, irritating their eyes, causing the eyes to matter and water. There are sprays on the market for keeping the flies away, but most horses are frightened by the sound of an aerosol spray, especially when too close to face and ears.

We've found that the most effective way to keep the flies from bothering the horses' eyes is to apply Nunn's Black Oil over the entire eyelid and surrounding area with a feather. The horse will close his eye when he sees the feather approaching and the oil can be applied liberally with practically no danger of getting any into the eye itself. Treatments every day or every other day are sufficient to alleviate the problem during the height of the fly season. Nunn's Black Oil is an old remedy and still a good one. It has been in use since 1873 and is a soothing dressing for saddle sores, cuts, cracks, scrapes, and the like, and it keeps the flies away from the sore. It is also a good hoof dressing.

Speaking of eye irritations, I once had an old bald-faced gelding whose eyes were badly irritated by sunlight during the summer. Most animals with white markings have pink skin beneath the white hairs. Black skin absorbs the sun's rays, but pink skin will sunburn. Pink skin also reflects the ultraviolet rays in sunlight— the rays which irritate

Applying black oil around the horse's eye with a feather, to keep face flies away. The horse closes his eye as the feather approaches.

The horse in these pictures is Nikki.

and damage the eye if accumulated in large doses. An eye sourrounded by pink skin will be much more irritated by sunlight than an eye surrounded by dark skin. I put black shoe polish around my gelding's eyes; the black absorbed the sunlight and seemed to help tremendously.

But back to the subject of influenza! This is a virus disease, highly contagious and hard to treat, for it does not respond to antibiotics. Antibiotics given to a horse with influenza are meant to prevent or control the secondary bacterial infections that follow the initial attack. When a horse is weakened by the virus, bacterial complications often follow, causing permanent damage in severe cases, or even deatĥ. Needless to say, it is much less costly to immunize your horses against influenza to begin with. Several vaccines are available. The one we use is two shots (two cc. per shot) two weeks apart, followed by a booster shot each year thereafter. These shots are given intramuscularly.

A couple of years ago we began vaccinating against strangles as well, another disease which our horses have never had, but which several horses in our area have gotten. Strangles is also known as distemper, catarrhal fever, and stable pneumonia. Unlike distemper of cats and dogs, which is caused by a virus, strangles (horse distemper) is caused by bacteria, *Streptococcus equi.* It is spread by direct contact, or by contaminated feed and water, and is rapidly spread by infected horses. It is usually picked up at public water troughs, mangers, etc., and is common at race tracks, stockyards, rodeo grounds, or any other place where many horses gather. About three days after exposure to this disease, there is a heavy discharge from the nose, and the horse snorts and coughs and has a fever. Lymph glands swell under the throat and jaws, causing difficult breathing. If not treated early these glands abscess, draining a yellow, creamy pus. Many complications can occur, including eye infection, internal abscesses, and infected joints. Some of these complications can prove fatal.

Because strangles is caused by bacteria it can be controlled very effectively with antibiotics and sulfa drugs if treated in the early stages. There is now a vaccine which will prevent strangles. Healthy horses over three months of age can be vaccinated. Three doses (ten cc. each) are given intramuscularly at weekly intervals. A yearly booster of one shot is given in the following years.

Strangles vaccine should never be given to a horse that has an active case of strangles or has the disease in the incubation stage. If there is any possibility your horse has already contracted strangles, *do not vaccinate.*

Strangles shots usually cause swelling and stiffness of the muscle tissue, but this can be partly prevented by exercise. It does no harm to ride the horse after a strangles vaccination; in fact, it will generally keep the swelling down and is recommended. Strangles and influenza both seem most prevalent in the fall in our part of the country, so we vaccinate in the summer.

We have never been bothered by tetanus in our area, but in the last few years we've heard of a couple of cases less than a hundred miles away. This may be something we will have to start vaccinating against also. Tetanus (lockjaw) is a disease that affects nearly all animals, particularly horses and man. The organism *Clostridium tetani* is found in the soil in most parts of the country. It can enter the horse whenever there is a wound or puncture in the skin. If the horse contracts this disease, symptoms appear two or three weeks (or even longer) after the wound which induced the infection, but by this time the disease is already well advanced. The first symptoms are difficulty in chewing and swallowing. The horse will stand stiff-legged, ears up and tail somewhat extended. The death rate for this disease is very high.

Tetanus vaccine can be given at any time, even to very young foals. The horse should receive two doses four to eight weeks apart, and receive an annual booster shot thereafter. If a wound occurs within two months after the first dose, the horse should receive an antitoxin. If a wound occurs following completion of the first year's vaccination program, a booster shot should be given immediately unless the last annual booster shot was given within the preceding three months.

Vaccinating horses every year can be a costly program, especially if you have quite a few horses, but losing a horse or having an epidemic run through them all can be even costlier. It pays to vaccinate, expensive as it may be. We've found that we can save considerable time and expense by giving the shots ourselves. We learned to give our own shots for several other reasons as well. We are a long way from a vet. Rather than having to make arrangements for a vet to come out to our ranch or taking the time to haul our horses to the veterinary clinic, we save time in instances where a few hours might make a difference in the recovery of the horse (in giving antibiotics, for example). Besides, giving shots is not difficult.

I'd like to tell you how we give shots. Perhaps not every horseman wants to try it himself, but for many horse owners—particularly those who own several horses—the convenience of being able to give your own shots can be worth a great deal. It is relatively simple, becoming easier with practice. And your own horses, who know and trust you, are good ones on which to learn. There are several techniques which make the procedure easier, and these I shall try to describe.

Most shots are given intramuscularly—deep into the muscle tissue. These are the easiest. Relatively few shots are given subcutaneously (just

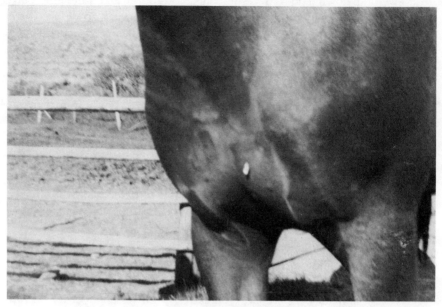

Giving a shot in the chest muscle. The needle is inserted in the pectoral muscle on either side of the breastbone. Avoid hitting the breastbone; it is in the center.

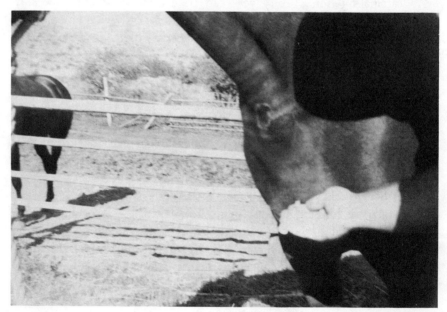

Then the syringe can be attached to the needle and the shot injected.

beneath the skin) or intradermally (between the layers of the skin). These are more tricky. Sleeping-sickness shots in particular (intradermal) should never be attempted until you've first had some instructions.

But intramuscular shots are easy. For these shots we use a relatively long needle, 1–1½ inches in length. An 18-gauge needle is large enough in diameter. Needles range in diameter from the tiny 26 to 22-gauge needles with which sleeping sickness shots are given, to 16-gauge and larger which we use to give shots to our cattle; cattle have a tougher hide and large shots are given more easily with a big needle.

Always use a sharp, straight needle. A dull needle will not go in as easily and the horse will feel more pain than with a sharp one. A bent needle is weakened and may break. Never take a chance on having a needle break off while it is in the horse. Straightening a bent needle only weakens it further, so if it is bent, throw it away.

One of the main things to remember when giving shots intramuscularly is to inject them into thick muscle and to avoid hitting a bone. Hitting a bone may bend your needle, but even worse, it hurts the horse and can cause an irritation on the bone.

We like to give shots in the chest muscle because the horse seems to be less sensitive here than on many other parts of the body. Also, the chest area is an easy place to work; the horse can be more easily controlled when you are working this close to his head. If a horse is nervous or unruly, shots are easier to give in the chest than in the rump, for he can't move his front end around as much, and you are less apt to get kicked. When giving shots in the chest, be careful not to strike the breastbone. Insert the needle into one of the big muscles on either side; the breastbone is in the center.

For large shots (anything more than 10 cc.), we prefer the heavy muscle covering either side of the horse's croup. With a nervous horse that is touchy about shots in the croup, a large shot can be split into two or three doses and given in the chest at two or three different sites. But shots given in the chest (especially large shots) are more apt to swell the tissues than shots given in the croup. The amount of swelling depends on the type of shot, and differs with various horses and their individual reactions to it. The swelling is unsightly and the horse may be a little sore and stiff, but it usually goes down to normal in a day or two.

On small foals we do not use the chest muscle; we give most shots in the muscle just below the buttock (the croup area is not always thick enough).

This is how we administer shots. First, we choose the needle and syringe we plan to use. Always use a syringe corresponding to the size of the shot. Syringes range in size from 1 or 2 cc. to 40 cc. or larger.

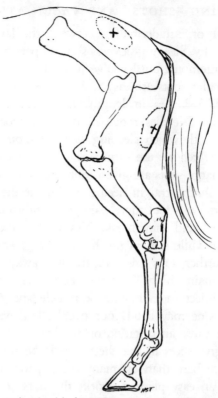

Areas for giving shots in the hindquarters. In the croup area . . . the large flat muscle on either side of the backbone; stay within the circle area and you will miss the hip bone. In the buttocks . . . you will not strike bones if you insert the needle into the thick muscle, neither too high nor too low.

If you are giving a small shot, use a small syringe. It will be more accurate and easier to read on the individual calibrations than a larger one.

Always disinfect the needle and syringe. Needles and glass-and-metal syringes can be boiled. Plastic syringes will not stand boiling, but can be washed thoroughly with warm soapy water, rinsed well, then rinsed with alcohol. It is best to use syringes that can be boiled. After use, the syringe should be washed out and boiled and kept in a clean place. We rinse ours in alcohol just before using it again. We also clean the area on the horse where we will give the shot. For this purpose we put some alcohol in a cup and make small cotton swabs (as many swabs as there are shots to give) to put in the cup to take out where we'll be vaccinating. We also like to use a different sterilized needle for each horse.

To fill the syringe, insert the needle through the rubber top of the vaccine bottle, tip the bottle upside down, then slowly pull the plunger to create a vacuum in the syringe. This vacuum will be filled by vaccine from the bottle. Pull the plunger slowly. Creating too much vacuum too quickly can break a syringe.

If you have a large bottle of vaccine and several horses to vaccinate, you will find that filling the syringe becomes harder each time because of the vacuum created in the bottle. It helps to insert air from the syringe into the bottle before you try to fill the syringe; the vaccine will come out much more easily. We generally do this when we have several horses to vaccinate and will be using up the entire bottle of vaccine. But it is not wise to insert air into a bottle that you plan to keep and use again at a later date, for this can contaminate the rest of the contents of the bottle—not with bacteria (the syringe has been sterilized and disinfected, and you should be using a sterile needle to fill the syringe each time; one needle can be kept aside for this purpose)—but perhaps with a minute trace of alcohol or water which might still be in the syringe. Alcohol or water may react with certain ingredients in the bottle (depending on the vaccine, the antibiotic, or the vitamins you are giving; some are water or alcohol base) and change its consistency or in other ways alter it so that it would not keep well.

When filling the syringe, avoid getting air into it. If you do have a little air in it after it is filled, hold the syringe in a vertical (needle straight up) position and press gently on the plunger until all the air has been pushed out. You must be careful not to push too hard or you will squirt out some of the vaccine as well.

Now you are ready to administer the shot. It is usually best to have the horse out in the open, rather than tied to a fence or in a stall; there is nothing to get in your way if he moves around a little. Have someone hold him for you. If the horse is nervous about shots, a blindfold works wonders. A blindfolded horse will usually stand quietly—he's afraid to move because he can't see where he is going—and since he can't see what's going on, he won't be aware of the exact moment of injection. It's in before he knows it. But do not use a blindfold on foals or young horses; it may frighten them. Some young horses lunge blindly around when they can't see, whereas an older horse will stand still.

If shots are given properly, the horse will not even flinch or jump. Swab the area with a piece of cotton soaked in alcohol to clean the place where you will insert the needle. Detach the needle from the syringe and, holding it firmly in your hand, thump the area soundly several times with the flat side of your fist. This thumping does not hurt the horse. It tends to desensitize the area and will mask the sensation of the needle. If you merely try to jab the needle in with no preparation, he will jump every time.

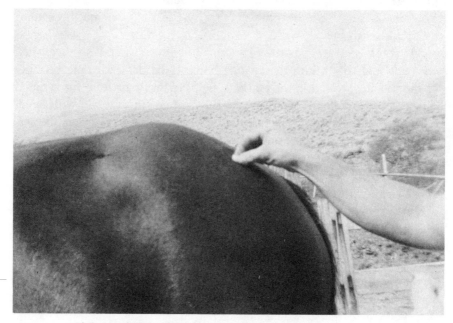

Giving a shot in the croup muscle.
1. Area is disinfected with cotton swab soaked in alcohol.

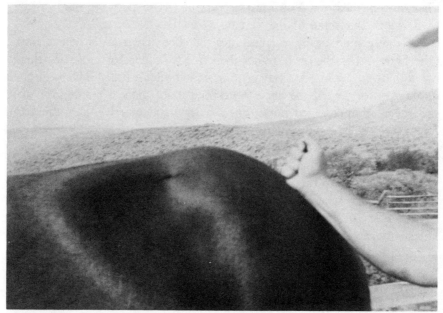

2. Needle is held between thumb and forefinger as the area is thumped with the flat of the fist in preparation for thrusting the needle into the muscle.

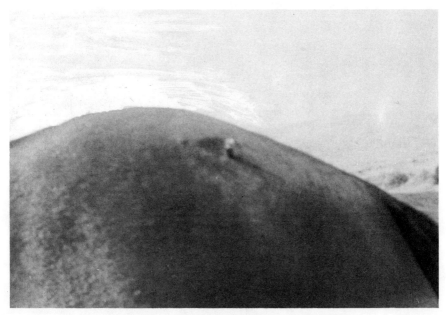

3. Needle is shown penetrating the muscle.

4. Syringe is attached to the needle . . .

5. . . . and the shot is administered.

After thumping several times, jab the needle in with the same rhythm. The mistake most beginners make is in not jabbing *hard* enough, and the needle does not get clear in—perhaps the beginner is more needle-shy than the horse! Remember, the faster the needle goes in, the less it will hurt; it will be in before the horse realizes it. If he does flinch or jump a little, by putting the needle alone in *first,* you can wait until he is calm and relaxed again before giving the shot. The syringe can then be reattached to the needle and the shot given.

I've seen beginners try to jab in the needle and syringe together, usually not getting the needle in deep enough, and then trying to give the shot to a jumpy, fighting horse, often ending up with the needle coming out in the process and spilling half the vaccine.

After giving the shot, the syringe and needle can be removed together. Sometimes a shot will ooze a little, but usually if you will press the area with your finger for a moment the oozing will stop.

The main advantage of putting the needle in first is that it is smoother and easier, and less likely to upset the horse because you can put it in quickly. Another advantage: you can tell whether or not you have hit a blood vessel *before* you inject the vaccine. *Never* put vaccine, antibotics, or vitamins directly into the blood stream. If you wait a few seconds before you attach the syringe to the inserted needle, you can tell whether you have struck a vein (arteries are located much deeper than veins; you are more likely to hit a vein than an artery)—the needle will begin to ooze and then to drip blood if you have. In this case, pull the needle out and try again in a different spot.

Another way to tell if you've hit a vein is to pull back on the plunger a little after the syringe is attached to the inserted needle. If blood appears in the syringe, remove the needle and syringe and try a different place.

One last suggestion. Teamwork helps. It's not impossible to give shots by yourself, especially to a horse that knows and trusts you, but it helps to have someone at the horse's head holding him still and reassuring him. The person at his head can often make all the difference, distracting him from the shot, and keeping him from moving at the wrong time.

Once in a great while a horse will have a reaction to a shot. There are two kinds of reactions, and a person should know the possibility of these so that he can call his vet if a severe reaction does occur. Sometimes a horse will have an allergic reaction to the vaccine. A reaction of this kind manifests itself in swelling or hives, and in severe cases, congestion of the lungs and shortness of breath (like an attack of asthma). If your horse has a bad allergic reaction to a shot, call your vet, who will take care of this problem with prompt medication to counteract the allegry. Allergic reaction is an individual horse's sensitivity to a particular type of shot and can occur even when the shot is given properly.

Another type of reaction occurs which is more severe, but is also rarer, for it generally occurs only when vaccine is administered improperly, producing a severe shock to the horse's system, as in the case of overdoses, injection of vaccine into the blood stream, or in giving shots of certain types to a horse that has already been sensitized (as in the case of vaccinating for a disease which the horse has already contracted). This reaction, called anaphylactic shock, is caused by an extreme sensitivity to the substance being injected, because the horse's system is already sensitized, either by the disease itself or by previous vaccine. When a horse suffers from anaphylactic shock he has sudden attacks similar to very severe allergic attacks, and may collapse (for his heart is affected) and die.

All vaccine bottles have a printed warning concerning the possibility of anaphylactic shock. The best way to avoid this reaction is to be sure to read the instructions for the vaccine and to give the shot properly, in the locations described and in the proper dosage, and to discuss the vaccination with your vet if you think the horse may have already contracted the disease; in some cases he will tell you not to give the vaccine. If vaccine is given properly, anaphylactic shock will almost never occur.

But if it ever does, call the vet *immediately*. If called in time, he can administer an antidote which may save your horse.

If you have never given shots before, you may wish to discuss the subject with your vet. He can tell you what diseases to vaccinate for in your area; he can supply you the vaccine or tell you where to buy it; he can show you how to give a shot, especially the tricky sleeping-sickness vaccination, and can tell you what precautions to take.

There is one last subject I would like to mention pertaining to our horses' health and a yearly vaccination program. My husband and I have found it very useful to keep health records on our horses. Undoubtedly, people who are in the business of raising and breeding horses keep records, in order to be accurate on breeding dates, foaling dates, and so forth, and probably they keep detailed health records, too. By the same token, many ranchers and cattle breeders keep excellent records on their livestock. But I want to point out the advantages of keeping good health records for the average horse owner—the person who owns one or more horses for pleasure, for sport or for show competition, or for ranching. Keeping good records can become a very handy and valuable practice over the years.

As horsemen, we want to learn all we can, especially about our own horses. Memory is not always reliable. There are times when we want to recall how we treated a certain ailment, how many cc. and what type of antibiotic we gave Nell when she was so badly wire cut, what we used to remove the proud flesh from Ginger's injured tendons, how long ago we vaccinated Nikki the first time for "lepto," how many cc. we gave in influenza vaccinations, and so on. It's surprising how often we want to look back and refer to some of that information.

In our records we put down the date and treatment of all health matters alongside the horse's name. We list the dates of all vaccinations. This is helpful in several ways. The dates are down in black and white and can aid a poor memory, insuring accuracy on shots which must be given at certain intervals apart. It's also handy to be able to look back to see when we gave the shots last year.

We write down any other treatments as well, such as the procedure we used to blister Nikki's knee (she ran a nail in her knee when she was a weanling, leaving a soft lump after the wound was healed), the way we treated Khamette's puncture wound in her foot, how we treated Nikki for "lepto" and doctored her eye for the opaque cornea which resulted from having "lepto," how I removed the lumps from Khamette's front legs when she was a yearling, how I treated rope burns on Nikki's hind pasterns, the treatment for Scrappy's dislocated stifle, what we used when Nell's foals scoured, and so forth.

Cases come up which we have never encountered before and we try to diagnose and treat them as best we can, perhaps trying several things. Years later we can look back when confronted with a similar case, and read the charts to discover what worked for us before. Anyone who has owned horses very long learns a great deal from experience, and we've found that our health records have become a good personal veterinary notebook. It's always a good idea to write down dosages and formulas, for it's alarming how easily a person forgets these things when he has no occasion to use them again for some time. Vets and some people who raise a lot of horses and work with great numbers of horses (people who see a variety of cases more often than we do) are well versed in the treatments they use often. But those of us who own just a few horses may encounter certain ailments just a few times in our lives, and then it is a great help to be able to look up the facts and figures we used before but have since forgotten.

These records can be especially important in emergencies when the vet is not available. And records are helpful in other ways also. When you do need veterinary assistance, it often can help the vet if you are able to tell him exactly how long the horse has had the problem, what treatments if any have already been given, and whether or not the horse has had this particular ailment before.

Our horses' health is extremely important—a sick or unhealthy horse is of no use to its owner. As conscientious horsemen we want to do our best to keep our animals healthy. We can do this by having a good yearly vaccination program for all infectious diseases in our area, worming the horses regularly, keeping our horses in the safest possible surroundings, taking no chances with health or safety. We can learn all we can about various ailments of horses and how best to treat them, learning to diagnose illness, how to give first aid, and how to treat the horse during his period of convalescence if he does become sick or injured. And we can keep accurate health records which can help to guide us in the future.

5

MISCELLANEOUS HEALTH PROBLEMS

In this chapter I want to touch on a few miscellaneous health problems which horsemen may encounter at one time or another. Let's touch on a couple of skin problems first—warts and ringworm.

Warts are found most often in young horses and usually appear around the muzzle—on the lips and nose. They are caused by a virus and can be spread from horse to horse. If left alone these warts usually disappear without treatment in a few months. If they become a real problem (if they interfere with the horse's breathing, for instance) they can be removed surgically. If they become a problem in a stable, or wherever many horses are apt to get them, a special vaccine can be prepared to immunize young horses against them.

Only one of our horses has ever had warts; Nikki wintered on a Montana ranch as a two-year-old one year when I was still in college, and she picked them up. She looked unsightly for a while with the little gray lumps all over her muzzle, but they went away without treatment before spring.

Ringworm is a skin disease caused by a fungus, and most kinds are contagious to other animals and to man. One of our horses (Bambi) had several ringworm lesions one winter when we had an outbreak of it among our cattle.

The ringworm fungus sends out spores, which start new infections when rubbed into the skin. In horses ringworm can be spread by infected brushes and curry combs, cinches and saddle blankets, etc. Young horses and horses deficient in vitamin A are more susceptible to the disease.

After the spores enter the skin, lesions are seen within a week to a month, appearing as circular areas in which the hair falls out or breaks off. Sometimes thick crusts form. There are several medicines you can get from your vet to treat ringworm and to keep it from spreading.

Now let's look at several ailments which are more serious—heaves, founder, and leptospirosis—the latter being a major cause of periodic ophthalmia, or "moon blindness" in horses.

Heaves is a disease of the lungs (chronic pulmonary alveolar emphysema). A horse with heaves has it for the rest of his life. When a horse has heaves, the millions of tiny air sacs in his lungs rupture and break down, creating a condition called emphysema.

A cough is the first noticeable symptom. The cough becomes worse when the horse is exercised or exposed to dust. Instead of getting better, this cough persists. The horse may have coughing fits after exercise, after drinking cold water, or when coming out of a warm stall into cold air.

When a horse has heaves, the lungs lose their normal elasticity and he has to force the air out as he breathes. In time he develops a big chest and a pot belly because the diaphragm muscles enlarge. He is short of breath and has no stamina.

Heaves are caused by infection or allergy. Some cases follow chronic bronchitis. Most cases seem to result when the horse is allergic to something he breathes, like dusty or moldy hay, dusty bedding, a dusty corral.

Heaves is a disease that gets progressively worse, but even though there is no cure for it, a careful horseman can help control the advance of the disease. A horse on good green pasture will have fewer symptoms than one fed hay. A horse with heaves should never be fed dusty or moldy hay. It is wise to avoid legume hay for a horse with heaves; it tends to contain more dust than well-cured grass hay. If you must feed hay, feed good grass and sprinkle it with water to settle any possible dust. Pelleted feeds are sometimes very helpful for horses with heaves. You can also buy a specially prepared ration in some localities for horses suffering from heaves.

If you ever have a horse with heaves, try to keep his environment as free of dust and mold as possible. Don't bed him on straw or any other material that might mold or be dusty. Wood shavings are preferable. Never work him on a full stomach; if you keep him from feed and water for several hours before you ride him, his stomach will not be so full and his lungs will have more room to expand. Never overwork him or overexert his lungs with too much running, climbing, etc. There are several drugs that can help relieve the horse. Your veterinarian can prescribe products that may be beneficial.

If a horse develops a cough, don't use him until it clears up. If it becomes severe or persistent, have a vet check him. Early cases of heaves properly cared for may assure many more years of usefulness for the horse.

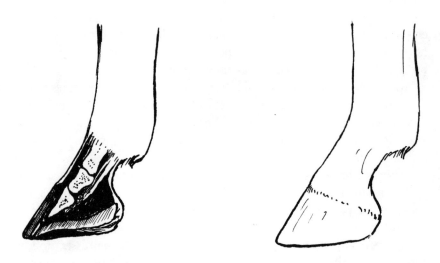

Normal foot (top), Chronic founder (bottom). Compare position of the bone and sole in the normal foot and the foundered foot.

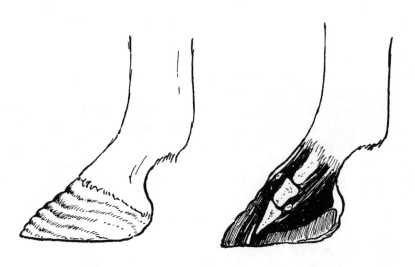

Now let's look at the problem of founder. Founder is a term used to describe the changes that occur in a horse's feet when he suffers a severe shock to his system. The hoofs can become very deformed. In most cases, founder is an unnecessary disaster. Founder can be prevented by proper care. Almost all cases of founder are the result of someone's neglect or ignorance.

To understand why founder can occur, let's look at the structures of the horse's feet. The horse's entire weight is supported by his four feet. Front legs bear more weight than hind legs. The bones and muscles of the horse's legs terminate inside the hoofs in an area that acts as a cushion and an attachment between the bones and tendons and the outer horny wall. This area is called the sensitive laminae. When the horse suffers a severe shock—an upset of his body chemistry—many changes take place in his body, including an increase in blood pressure and congestion of blood in certain blood vessels. He develops a fever. Usually the congested blood vessels do not cause serious or permanent damage in other parts of his body, only in the hoofs, which are encased in solid walls; the congestion and swelling create great pressure and terrible pain, permanently damaging the sensitive inner tissues—the laminae. That's why founder is called laminitis; it is an inflammation of the sensitive laminae.

When this happens, the pain makes it difficult for the horse to walk. Lameness shows up first in the front feet because they carry most of the horse's weight. After the fever leaves, the congestion and changes in the horse's body gradually return to normal, but permanent damage has been done to the feet and they become increasingly deformed. The sole drops down, the laminae separate, and the hoof wall appears ringed and ridged.

Here are some of the causes of founder. All, you will notice, are the result of some kind of stress or strain or imbalance that upsets the body chemistry.

1. Overfeeding, especially rich feeds and grains.

2. Drinking cold water when overheated. *Never* let a horse take a big drink when he is working hard or is hot and sweaty. The blood rushes to his stomach to try to maintain an even temperature, and the muscles and extremities that have been working so hard and are in desperate need of repair and fresh blood are neglected; the horse's whole system is thrown into a state of confusion.

3. The same thing can happen any time the horse's temperature is drastically upset—whenever there are rapid changes from one extreme to another—as when an overheated horse is washed with cold water, or left to cool rapidly after hard use on a cold or wet day, or has to stand in a cold wind when he is hot and sweaty, etc. Sudden chilling of large areas of the horse's body sends blood rushing to these parts to keep them

warm. There is only so much blood, and some part of the anatomy has to suffer. Any time that the horse's system has to make a rapid change, his carefully balanced control mechanisms are thrown awry. When the horse is chilled drastically in this manner, the result may be a bad cold or even worse—pneumonia or founder.

4. Grass founder is another example of the horse's system suffering an upset by too sudden change. Grass founder occurs when a horse on dry feeds is suddenly allowed to eat a large amount of new green grass. A horse will not get grass founder if he is changed gradually to the new green feed—allowed to graze only a short time the first day, a little longer the second, and so on.

5. Concussion caused by riding on hard surfaces, particularly pavement. This puts a great deal of strain on the sensitive areas of the horse's feet (they are forced to absorb too much of the shock) and may cause him to founder, especially if he is carrying too much weight.

6. Increased weight on the feet can also cause founder. When a horse is lame in one foot and tries to carry most of his weight on the other for long periods of time, he may founder in his good foot. Founder can also occur when a horse is extremely overweight, or when a horse shifts his weight back and forth (as when traveling at sea). An overweight pregnant mare is susceptible to founder, especially if she gets no exercise and stands for long periods of time.

7. Extreme exhaustion can cause founder, especially if the horse is out of condition. Extreme exhaustion will send the animal into shock which, if severe enough, may cause death.

8. Severe infections that go untreated can also cause founder, such as pneumonia, or infection of a mare's uterus after foaling.

9. Heat stroke.

10. Drastic laxatives which upset the horse's system.

Here are some good rules to follow that can help keep your horse from foundering.

1. Condition him gradually, never working him to the point of exhaustion.

2. When a horse is hot or tired from working, limit the amount of water he drinks (just a few swallows) and do not feed him much at all until he is completely cooled (dried off, and heartbeat, breathing and temperature back to normal).

3. Cool a horse *slowly* after using him—by walking him, blanketing him or brushing him vigorously, drying him off and protecting him from cold breezes until he is completely cooled and dry.

4. Always introduce any new feeds slowly, over a period of several days.

5. Always feed him a balanced ration, and never overfeed him.

If a horse becomes foundered, prompt treatment should be given to relieve his pain and to try to keep the feet from suffering permanent damage. Call your veterinarian immediately.

Keep the horse's feet cold and wet, and relieve the strain on his feet by giving him soft footing. The "soaking" treatment in a wet mud pit has been used for many years and is still an effective way to relieve the pain, but now there are drugs (antihistamine and cortisone) that can relieve the pain more quickly.

Many horses with founder (deformed feet) are not too seriously affected and can still be useful if shod correctly with special shoes. Some experimentation and research has been done by Dr. M. P. Mackay-Smith (a veterinarian well known for his work with horses), who has found that the hoof changes are caused by alterations in the hoof horn during the early stages of founder. His treatment of founder is to keep the horny hoof wall from bearing weight during these early stages, by removing or rasping away excess horn and transferring the weight to the sole. This treatment tends to let the horny wall grow back normally, and completely prevents the deforming hoof changes in many early cases of founder. The rate of recovery and the completeness of recovery depend of course on the severity of the case and on how much time has elapsed before treatment was started. As with many other ailments, prevention is by far the best cure. Using and caring for your horses wisely is the best insurance against founder.

Leptospirosis, or "lepto" as it is called by cattlemen in our part of the country, is a disease caused by a bacteria—a spiral-shaped germ called a leptospirochete. There are many, many kinds; some cause disease in dogs, others in cattle, pigs, and horses, others in wild animals, others in humans. In humans it can be serious (Weil's disease) or mild, depending upon the type of leptospirochete that causes it.

There are two main types of leptospirochete, the nonpathogenic (harmless) type which live and multiply in standing fresh water, ponds, lakes, and so forth, and the pathogenic types which live and multiply mainly in the tissues of animals. Once outside the body, these harmful organisms do not live very long, depending on the temperature and moisture.

Leptospirosis is not a common disease among horses, and it affects individual horses differently. But I want to mention it here because it is time more horsemen were aware that this disease exists and that it *can* affect horses.

Lepto was first introduced into our part of the country by cattle that were brought in from other areas. For about twelve years now we have vaccinated our cattle against this disease every year, for if lepto goes through a herd, the economic loss to the rancher is great. Lepto causes the cows to abort their calves.

A "carrier" is an animal that contracts the disease, recovers, and still harbors leptospires in its body that can be spread to other animals. Rodents are the prime carriers of many kinds of lepto. Pigs are the main carriers of *Leptospira pomona,* the species that is the most common problem in livestock, including horses and cattle. There is a vaccine which will immunize livestock, including horses, against *L. pomona.*

When a horse gets lepto he may or may not appear sick. Individual horses react differently. He may have many symptoms, or he may have only one or two. Lepto is a very versatile bacterium; it can localize almost anywhere and cause trouble. The leptospirochete may infect the entire body, causing fever, depression, lethargy, lack of appetite, and sometimes jaundice. Pregnant mares may abort. The body in general is often able to combat the disease—horses rarely die from lepto—but the leptospirochetes may cause further problems in the kidney, the eye, or the joints.

Lepto can be transmitted to a susceptible animal through contact with any secretions or excretions from infected animals—urine, nasal and eye discharges, saliva, etc. Lepto can live for many days in damp or saturated soil, but dies within a few hours on dry soil. It can't stand dehydration or sunlight.

Blood tests will tell if a horse has been exposed to the disease, but are not always conclusive in whether or not the horse has an active infection. Only the isolation of the germ from the blood or urine or other body fluids is positive proof of the active disease. Blood tests can tell a person the amount of reaction in the horse's blood serum to the lepto antigen (a very high titer that is steadily rising should make a person suspicious of active infection, but it is not positive proof because other factors can make the titer rise). Many healthy horses that have never had any obvious symptoms of lepto show a blood titer, indicating that they have come in contact with the disease at one time. Any horse that has been vaccinated against lepto will also show a titer.

Lepto is thought to be one of the major causes of periodic ophthalmia in horses, a disease of the eye that has been known since the fourth century and which was called moon blindness because horsemen mistakenly thought the recurring attacks were related to phases of the moon. Periodic ophthalmia is also called recurrent iridocyclitis and uveitis.

When a horse has periodic ophthalmia, the first symptoms are usually a watering of one or both eyes. The pupil constricts, the eye is sensitive to light, and there is conjunctivitis (inflammation). The cornea may become opaque (cloudy and bluish—gray) at this time or at a later date. These attacks last for indefinite periods of time, then the eye clears up, only to have the problem recur from time to time, anywhere from a month later to a year or longer. Each attack further damages the interior parts of the eye and in almost all cases blindness eventually results. Sometimes the other eye becomes involved also. Periodic ophthalmia is the most common cause of blindness in horses.

Some years ago periodic ophthalmia was blamed on a riboflavin deficiency, but current thought emphasizes other causes. There may be several causes—leptospirosis, streptococcus infections (such as strangles), and parasitic larvae that lower the resistance of the eye. Periodic ophthalmia is not highly contagious and seems to be caused by several factors acting together or separately. One theory is that repeated attacks of any or several of the causative factors result in a progressively greater reaction in the eye.

Many outbreaks of lepto in horses have been seen in the United States and other countries, but often a horse with lepto has no eye involvement. Usually lepto is a fairly mild disease in horses, and when the horse recovers he is no longer a "carrier." His blood will, however, carry antibodies and a blood test will show a titer for lepto.

There is no real cure for periodic ophthalmia, but an attack can be treated to relieve the horse's pain. Effective treatment can help postpone blindness. The horse should be put in a dark stall or barn until the attack subsides, to rest the eye and relieve pain caused by bright sunlight. If the horse has lepto, high levels of streptomycin and broad-spectrum antibiotics can help control that aspect of his problem. Isolate him so he won't spread it to other horses in the early stages, or vaccinate other horses that might come in contact with him or his excreta or with water he may have contaminated.

Although we have vaccinated our cows against this disease for many years, I had never heard of it in horses until one of our own mares, Nikki, provided us with firsthand experience. The summer of 1966 she had an irritation of her left eye at two different times. It watered and she held it partly closed. The irritation cleared up and I thought no more about it until the next spring when her eye suddenly became cloudy. I put her in a dark barn, treated the eye three times daily, and a veterinarian diagnosed her problem as lepto.

Throughout that summer Lynn and I doctored her for lepto and for the periodic ophthalmia, giving her hundreds of injections (including antibiotics, vitamins—particularly vitamin A—and a nonspecific protein treatment that was meant to help clear up the clouded cornea). The eye varied in usefulness that summer. Sometimes she had vision in it, some-times she didn't. I had to be careful when approaching her, always speak-ing to her first before I touched her on the blind side to keep from startling her. At times it bothered her very much, so I fashioned a blinder to cover the eye, using an old towel and a halter, to keep the sunlight out. We had let her out of the dark barn and back with the other horses, for the "solitary confinement" was making her lonely, nervous and ir-ritable.

By late summer she was much better and I began to ride her again. We continued giving her injections of vitamin A through that fall and winter. Needless to say, she became very much accustomed to being "doctored."

The eye remains cloudy to this day, but she sees out of it still, though not as well as she should. The cloudiness varies. Some days the cornea is clearer than on others, and I have come to feel that environmental condi-tions affect it—wind, dust, moisture in the air, etc. The pupil has been affected, for it remains somewhat constricted even in dim light, interfering with Nikki's night vision. So far her "bad eye" has not hindered her use-fulness; she is surefooted and handles herself well in rough country, but a rider must be careful with her in heavy timber. She is more apt to run into branches on the defective side. I ride her so much that I am prepared for her excessive spookiness at night (when coming home after dark from riding range), and instinctively "look out for her" on her left side in dense brush or timber, but I would not want anyone riding her who was not aware of her problem.

Up to the time I write this, she has had no further attacks (it has been more than a year and a half now), but I realize that the eye may become worse at any time and that she might eventually become blind. I just hope that it will not happen soon, for she is one of our best mares, and an excellent stock horse. But we shall continue to use and enjoy her as long as we can.

Because of our experiences with Nikki, we've tried to learn all we could about lepto and periodic ophthalmia, to find out how serious these problems can be, how to treat Nikki, and how to protect our other horses. It was not easy to find accurate information on these problems; not many horsemen are aware of them, and much research still needs to be done. It was frustrating to be confronted by such vastly differing opinions on leptospirosis, ranging from the opinion that lepto is a mild, self-limiting disease in horses, to the other extreme that Nikki should be destroyed because of possibilities she would remain a "carrier" for the rest of her life. Because I value my mare highly, I was led on a desperate search for accurate information. The facts presented on leptospirosis in this chapter are in keeping with the theories and research on this disease up to date.

Lepto in horses is most common east of the Rocky Mountains, but it is becoming more common in the West than horsemen realize. Since it is often a mild disease in horses, some horsemen are never aware that their horses contract it unless it produces serious side effects such as abortion or periodic ophthalmia.

Because periodic ophthalmia is such a serious disease, eye irritations in horses should never be overlooked. Proper care and treatment can make a great difference in the future usefulness and vision of the affected horse. When in doubt about the causes of an eye problem, contact your veterinarian immediately.

Perhaps you will never have firsthand experience with lepto or periodic ophthalmia. I hope you never do. But it is my hope that more horsemen will become aware of these problems and the facts concerning them, so that they will not be caught off guard and in the dark as we were. If our experiences can save even one horseman the agony and frustration we went through with Nikki, it will have been worth it.

6

DOCTORING MINOR WOUNDS

One morning in early spring when I went out to feed our horses, I discovered that Fahleen, our weanling filly, had injured a hind leg. Somewhere in our pasture she had run into something sharp and had gouged a nasty hole just below her hock on the inside of the leg. The wound had bled quite a bit but had stopped bleeding by the time I went out to feed the horses. Raw flesh and tendon were exposed.

I gave a silent groan of dismay. What a time she had picked to get herself in a scrape! She had never had any kind of injury before and this would be her first experience of being "doctored." Knowing her high-strung nature and proud disposition, I rather dreaded the ordeal, for I was very pregnant with our first child (the baby was due in less than a week) and not up to much of a tussle.

I got her in, thankful for the way her daily handling—we had been graining her daily—had made her fairly trusting and manageable. And she didn't mind having her legs handled; I had trimmed her feet regularly and groomed her occasionally. But putting medicine that stings on a wound that hurts was a different story. Having the wound on the inside of the leg, hard to reach, made things even more difficult.

Lynn held her for me and tied up her front foot. A horse generally won't kick with the hind foot that's on the same side as the front one that's up, because of the balance problem, but he *can,* and Fahleen did. I finally managed to get the medicine on by bracing my head in her flank as one does with a kicking milk cow to help immobilize that leg, and by pushing firmly on the leg to keep her from getting it far enough forward to clobber me when she *did* get it off the ground to kick. We moved around the barnyard quite a bit but we got the medicine on with no further casualties.

A few days later our son Michael was born, and Lynn doctored

A wound on the inside of the leg is hard to reach.

Fahleen with my father's help while I was in the hospital. And about the first thing I did upon returning home five days later was—you guessed it —doctor that filly.

Some horses accept unpleasant situations more unwillingly than others. Maybe some have a greater sensitivity to pain. I don't know. I do know that old Nell and all her offspring, including Fahleen, are very sensitive animals and usually put up quite a bit of resistance to anything that hurts, bothers, or just rubs them wrong, especially until they gain a great deal of confidence in the person handling them—usually a process of several years. Horses are individuals and will react differently to the various problems that arise in doctoring. What works well for one might not work at all for another. By trial and error, experimenting, and by getting to know each horse individually under trying situations, you will eventually discover the methods that work best for each horse.

There are two problems in treating wounds. First is knowing the proper treatment to give (and you might need a veterinarian to help you with this), and second is the problem of administering it. In this chapter I'd like to discuss these problems and the treatment of minor wounds in general.

The horse is a fairly intelligent animal, but he is not always smart enough to avoid trouble or to extricate himself once he blunders into it. Nature made him an animal of the wide open spaces, but man and our modern world have booby-trapped him with unnatural barriers, barbed wire, nails, pipes, and just plain "junk" which can injure him. Although the conscientious horseman tries his best to make fences and enclosures smooth and safe, now and again a horse will injure himself.

I've always said that barbed wire and horses don't mix, for it seems that most of the injuries our horses have received over the years have been wire cuts. It would be so wonderful to have pole or board fences, but here on our strung-out mountain ranch we have more than twelve miles of fence, and the cost, labor, and problem of transporting fencing materials up the steep hills (some of which are too steep even for a jeep to climb) make anything but wire fence practically out of the question.

But there are some general rules about wire fences that usually hold true. A horse that grows up in barbed wire will respect the wire and not tangle with it under ordinary circumstances, whereas a horse accustomed to nothing but pole or board fence may not see the wire and run into it, or may try to jump it. Also, a well-kept tight fence will not be so apt to injure your horse as a loose, saggy one. A horse won't be so apt to reach through a good tight fence, and even if he does, he's not as liable to get a foot caught as he is in a saggy one. There are exceptions to every rule, of course, and these are the times we are confronted by an injury to doctor—like the time Ginger was frightened by lightning and tried to leap a wire fence, tearing the skin from both knees; the time Nell went through a fence, cutting her pasterns to the bone; the time the horses were running in the pasture when snow was melting and slushy and Bambi couldn't turn in time to miss the fence and slid right into it; or the time Nikki lay down and rolled too close to a fence and got her feet caught in it.

Whenever a horse is injured, we should be able to judge the seriousness of the injury and how to treat it, if we can do so without veterinary assistance. The following list of items might be called a "first-aid kit" for horses. We generally keep most of these on hand in our tack room on a special shelf.

1. A sulfa powder or other antibiotic powder, or sulfa-base ointment.
2. Boric acid for use as a mild eyewash.
3. A fly-repellent dressing.
4. Scarlet Oil or some similar heavy liquid medication for deep wounds that need to grow new flesh.
5. Picric acid or some other suitable medication for retarding growth of proud flesh.

6. Old sheets torn in strips and rolled for bandages.
7. Squeeze bottles—old ketchup, cosmetic, or even dish-detergent squeeze bottles. These are good for squirting warm water into a wound to cleanse it. The smaller bottles are handy container-applicators for powdered or liquid medicines.
8. Iodine, for puncture wounds of the *foot. Never* use iodine or other strong medications such as methylene blue on an open wound. These burn the tissues; the flesh may slough away, leaving a scar. A deep wound that has been treated with iodine or methylene blue cannot be closed or sutured for it will fester and abscess. Iodine should be used only for treating thrush, puncture wounds of the foot, and ringworm. It is also good for disinfecting the navel of a newborn foal.
9. Other useful items in our tack room are: a hoof pick, hoof knife, twitch, scissors, and fencing tool (to free a horse caught in wire).

The first step in treating a wound is diagnosing the extent of the injury. Can we treat it ourselves or will it require the aid of a vet? Injuries such as broken bones, deep gashes that require suturing, an injured joint that has lost its fluid, etc., are problems best handled by a veterinarian. The second step, in localities where tetanus exists, is to give the horse a tetanus shot if his are not up to date. To be effective, a tetanus shot must be given within 24 hours of the wound's occurrence.

In general, these are the steps we follow in treating a wound, remembering that a wound must heal from the inside out. First we clean the wound, especially if it has dirt or mud or matted flesh and hair in it. Squirting with warm soapy water and rinsing thoroughly is usually effective. Then we apply an antibiotic, or healing medication, the kind depending on the type and severity of the wound. In deep or severe wounds we also give the horse an injection of antibiotics to help combat infection. Then we treat the wound daily until it has healed. With proper care, even serious wounds can be healed up with very little scar tissue to mar the horse's looks. In deep cuts on the lower legs (below the hock and knee) proud flesh—an unsightly rubbery growth—may develop if tendons are injured. This exuberant growth is the result of an injured tendon growing profusely to try to repair itself. In these types of injuries, consult your vet for medication. He will usually tell you to use a healing medication for the first few days to help the new flesh grow, then give you picric acid or some other preparation to use that will retard the growth of proud flesh until the wound is healed. If proud flesh once gets started it is very hard to get rid of. It can be done, but it takes much time and trouble.

If a wound is bleeding profusely, your first step is to stop the loss of

Squeeze bottles are handy for applying medication.

blood. If it is not bleeding badly, put a clean cloth over the wound and simple blood clotting will soon stop the flow. But if a major vein or artery has been cut, more drastic measures must be taken. A cut vein flows steadily and the blood is deep red. A cut artery flows bright red and the blood spurts each time the heart beats. When our yearling Fahleen stuck a front foot through the fence by pawing at the wire she made no gaping wound but apparently pricked the side of her foot deeply enough to hit an artery; within minutes her belly and hind legs were red-spattered from the spurting blood.

In case of a cut artery, apply pressure between the wound and the heart. With a cut vein, apply pressure on the side of the wound away from the heart, for the vein is bringing blood to the heart. I stopped Fahleen's bleeding by wrapping strips of an old sheet around the foot in many layers, making a mild pressure bandage.

In extreme cases, when the horse is losing a great deal of blood from a cut artery, a tourniquet may have to be used. But before going this far, try a pressure bandage; a tourniquet can do permanent damage by cutting off the blood supply to the limb, if applied too tight or too long. If you must use one, do so with care, tightening slowly until the flow of blood stops, and no tighter. In twenty minutes or less, loosen it and let the blood flow for a minute or so before tightening again. Failure to release the tourniquet at intervals will kill the tissues from lack of blood. The tourniquet should be applied between the wound and the heart.

We've never had to resort to a tourniquet on our own horses; we've been able to stop bleeding by other means. In some cases the bleeding had stopped on its own by the time we discovered the injured horse. Bleeding will usually stop eventually, but may leave the horse weak from loss of blood. And a horse *can* bleed to death if the cut is severe enough.

A pressure bandage can be made by placing a roll of bandage or a hard object such as a piece of wood or rock (wrapped and padded with clean cloth) against the cut, then bandaging firmly with bandage or strips of sheet. Continue wrapping until the bleeding stops; it will usually take many layers. Old sheets torn in three-inch strips are good for bandaging. Leave the bandage in place until the vet arrives. If the vet is not available and you are treating the wound yourself, clean the wound thoroughly before applying the pressure bandage. Usually a wound that is bleeding profusely will tend to clean itself out, but any mud or dirt or hair should be removed; a quick rinse won't take long. Leave the bandage on for several days if the gash is a bad one, and it should start to heal properly if it was cleaned beforehand to prevent infection.

Nail wounds should always have special attention. A puncture is sometimes hard to see, and hard to treat. This type of wound usually does not bleed much. If it is not seen and treated it will heal from the outside first, leaving a pus pocket underneath that may abscess and send infection throughout the horse's system. To treat a nail wound you must first open up the hole and clean it out with hydrogen peroxide or some other good disinfectant (*not* iodine) recommended by your vet. Then put a piece of sterile cotton soaked in antiseptic into the wound. This dressing should be changed daily until the wound has healed from the inside out. If the wound is not recent or has started to abscess by the time you discover it, the horse may need antibiotics.

Usually when a horse is hurt, he is also frightened. He doesn't know what is happening and he may not realize you are trying to help him. All he knows is that he hurts and that your poking around hurts even more; he may try to fight the treatment. If he is very frightened or in much pain, it is wise to use some means of restraining him to keep him from hurting you or himself further in his efforts to get away from the treatment.

In treating an injured horse, it is easiest to have two people, one to hold the horse (using a halter and lead rope—a bridle is not adequate; you want control of the horse without fussing with his mouth) and to distract him, and the other to apply the medication. It's not impossible to treat a horse alone, but it's a lot easier with two. Then the horse won't have to be tied. We never like to tie a horse when he's being doctored. If he is hurt or frightened he may pull back and injure himself. Also, if he's tied to a fence, the fence can get in your way; he may push you against it. It's better to have an open place with lots of room to work. Never try to treat a horse that is loose. Always have his head under control.

We never stand directly in front of a horse we are working with. Some horses are apt to strike when they are upset and annoyed. Don't be in the way. It is best to stand at the shoulder, and better to be close than to be some distance away. Even if a horse moves suddenly you won't be so apt to be knocked down or kicked or jumped on if you are close and braced against the horse and ready to move *with* him. And a good rule to remember about kicking: only if you are at a distance from the horse will you get the full force of a kick, so stay close.

Never be directly in front of a knee when bending down to treat the lower part of the front leg or even just to apply a hoof dressing or to trim a fetlock. A horse can hit you in the face with his knee even without meaning to if he happens to pick up his foot. I know of a vet who lost an eye this way.

Speaking in a calm and soothing voice helps to pacify the horse. Shouting "Whoa!" only makes him more nervous. Jiggling the lead rope can help distract him. So will a firm hand on his shoulder or neck. I like to hold onto the horse firmly at the top of his neck above the withers with the hand that's not holding the halter, while I speak to him soothingly. This helps keep his attention and holds him still.

A twitch is sometimes helpful as a restraint. It can be made from an old shovel handle or a similar piece of wood about a foot long. A hole is drilled in one end and a leather thong put through the hole and tied to form a loop about six inches long. Sometimes the situation arises in which you need a means to make the horse stand still for shots or doctoring; a twitch can be used for this purpose on most horses. Slip the loop over his upper lip and gradually twist it tight. He will concentrate on the pain in his nose and will forget about what you are doing to treat his wound. One person should hold the twitch while the other person treats the horse. There are many gentle horses that are just fussy and fidgety enough to make doctoring them difficult, and a twitch can often solve this problem.

Proper twitching will not make the horse head-shy. When you are done, release the twitch slowly and then gently massage the lip. Many horses will stand still when twitched, but not all. Some horses (we have a couple) fight the twitch as well as the treatment. For most of our horses we have come to prefer a blindfold. This will usually do the trick, but in a few instances we also tie up a front foot if we need to immobilize them further.

A blindfolded horse will usually stand quietly; he's afraid to move

Blindfold consisting of four clothespins and a folded towel.

because he can't see where he's going. A few years ago my father thought of a clever way to put on a blindfold and we've used it ever since because it works so well. We put it on with clothespins.

We've used blindfolds for many years in doctoring some of our nervous and fidgety horses, but the clothespin idea was an innovation that works much better than the other ways we've tried. With clothespins the blindfold can be put on and off very easily and quickly. Before, we always used a grain sack or a jacket, but then there was the problem of tying it on or stuffing it under the halter, which in itself can be difficult with a nervous horse. Sometimes the floppy sack or jacket would spook him while we were trying to put it on, or it might begin to slip off before we were through doctoring or giving the shot.

But now we use an old towel folded double or triple, just the right size to fit the face area, pinned onto the halter with four clothespins. It can be pinned on one side securely without flapping or frightening the horse, then it can be spread across his face in one easy motion without scaring him, and pinned on the other side. The clothespins hold very well unless the horse can rub them against something such as a fence, and they come off easily and quickly when you are ready to remove the blindfold. You can then take it off in one smooth motion without startling him. The old jacket or grain sack we used before usually flopped a little

Blindfolded and front leg tied up. . . . When these pictures were taken I was treating a wire cut on Nikki's hind leg.

in the breeze when taking it off because it couldn't come off all at once very easily.

The summer that we treated Nikki continually for lepto and periodic ophthalmia we gave her many injections, vaccine, vitamins, antibiotics, serums to help the eye condition—often a shot or two each day. At first she was nervous and it was impossible to give her a shot without her fighting us. Blindfolding her made the task much easier. Eventually she became so accustomed to having shots that we no longer needed a blindfold. All the shots and handling we gave her made her a much calmer and more trusting horse. One word of caution about blindfold: Don't use them on foals or young horses. A young horse is more apt to plunge around blindly in fright if he can't see, whereas an adult horse will usually stand still.

If on some occasion you need more restraint, you may need to use hobbles or to tie up a foot. It is always good to carry a pocket knife so that if anything goes wrong you could cut the horse free from a rope that might be choking him or restraining him in a dangerous position. A hind leg can be tied up to keep the horse from kicking, but some horses will throw themselves with a hind leg tied up. For most injuries we have found a front leg tied up to be easier and altogether adequate. You need good judgment in using restraints. Take into consideration where the horse is injured. Will the restraint you use make his injury worse or start the wound bleeding again? Always try to think of the best way to control and handle the horse without his fighting the restraint and further hurting himself.

Before leaving this chapter on treating wounds, I'd like to discuss puncture wounds in the horse's foot. Puncture wounds anywhere in the horse's body are always serious because they can lead to tetanus, but a puncture wound in the foot can be very bad, for it may damage the inner tissues and cause any one of several serious problems—inflammation of the bone, a fracture, decay of the pedal bone, or decay of the digital cushion. A puncture in the middle third of the frog is very serious because it may puncture the navicular bursa.

A puncture wound in the foot is not always easy to locate, as I discovered one winter with Khamette. She had been wintering with several other horses in a 320-acre pasture in the mountains. On one ride up to check on them, I noticed she was lame in the right front leg. Examination of the foot revealed nothing except that her hoofs were too long. I rode

Weanling Nikki with inner-tube "boot" on her front leg to keep her from chewing and biting at her knee, which we were treating with a "blister" to reduce swelling (soft lump) caused by a nail wound.

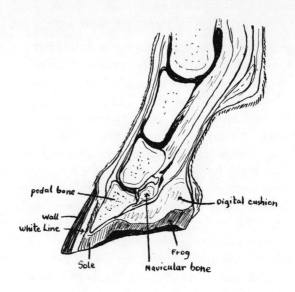

pedal bone
Wall
white Line
Sole
Navicular bone
Frog
Digital cushion

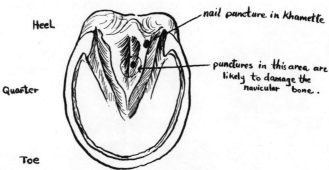

Heel
Quarter
Toe
nail puncture in Khamette
punctures in this area are
likely to damage the
navicular bone.

Cross section of Horse's Foot. (Courtesy *The Western Horseman*)

back to the ranch to get some shoeing tools and returned to remove her shoes and trim her feet. The hoof, sole, and frog of her lame foot appeared normal. Her lameness puzzled me for I could find nothing wrong in the foot, leg, or shoulder. I attributed the lameness to an old wound scar on the side of her foot above the coronary band; it looked scraped and I thought perhaps she had struck it with another foot or bruised it on the rocky mountainside.

When I rode back up there the next day to see how she was doing, her lameness was much more pronounced; unknowingly I had made it worse by taking her shoes off and trimming her feet, putting more of her weight directly onto the sore area. I led her down out of the mountains and trailered her the rest of the way to the ranch for further observation.

Swelling had started above the fetlock joint and there was quite a bit of heat, but there was no pain associated with the swelling. Snakebite and strain were ruled out.

The possibility of a puncture wound entered my mind but didn't seem likely, first because the mountain pasture she was in was free of nails and junk as far as I knew, and second because an examination of the bottom of her foot revealed nothing. There were no cracks in the white line or black spots in the sole. When examining a horse for a puncture wound, these cracks or black spots should be trimmed or probed to their full depth to see if any of them lead into sensitive tissue and are the cause of the infection. And none of the shoe nails had gone into sensitive tissue; I checked out all the old nail holes when trimming her foot. Her frog appeared normal, too. In trimming it I could discover no puncture holes.

So I didn't discover the true nature of her lameness until drainage began at the bulb of her heel. When infection is present in the foot, drainage will break out at the coronary band near the heel if the wound itself has no drainage. When Khamette's heel began to drain I realized there *must* be a wound somewhere in the foot. So even though I had already trimmed the frog, I trimmed it again with renewed determination. When I had trimmed it down fully half its original depth I discovered what

Khamette standing patiently soaking her foot in bucket of hot Epsom salts solution.

Khamette with protective rubber boot on her injured foot.

until now I hadn't dug down far enough to find—a perfectly round hole the size of a small nail or roofing tack. The spongy material of the frog had closed up again after the nail had made its hole, leaving no sign of the puncture.

I carved down deeper at the site of the nail hole and came to a pus pocket that had hollowed out quite a bit of the base of the frog. I cut away some of the tissue so that the infection would have adequate drainage. Ideally, a puncture wound should be treated immediately after it occurs; it should be opened to drain, soaked, cleaned with disinfectant, and the hole plugged with a wick of some sort that will allow drainage. A puncture wound in the sole should be opened so that there is at least a quarter-inch hole into the infected tissue, with the walls of the drainage hole widening toward the ground surface of the sole so that it won't become obstructed. When the wound is in the frog, the frog should be trimmed away at the site of the puncture until adequate drainage is established.

After thoroughly cleaning Khamette's foot, I soaked it in magnesium sulfate solution (Epsom salts dissolved in hot water). For this I used a plastic bucket and made sure the water was not so hot as to cause discomfort. From time to time I added additional hot water as the solution cooled. I wasn't sure whether she would stand still with her foot in the bucket, but she was very patient about the whole thing. Perhaps the soaking was soothing to the soreness.

After soaking the foot, I poured some iodine into the puncture wound, plugged it with vaseline to keep the iodine in, and bandaged her hoof in clean rags. I made a boot for her out of an old tire inner-tube, using leather straps to hold it in place. This was to keep the wound clean, for melting snow had made the pasture very wet and muddy.

Once healing is well begun, it is not necessary to soak and bandage the wound every day—every two or three days is sufficient—but it is very important that the wound be kept clean and dry until it is healed. I soaked Khamette's foot daily for a week, changing the bandages each

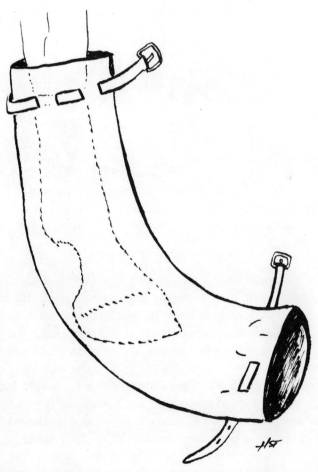

Boot made from old inner-tube and leather straps. (Courtesy *The Western Horseman*)

Hoof in boot. Fold up the end and secure it around the pastern. Twist top around cannon until it is tight, and fasten strap. If inner tube is stiff and sturdy, boot will not slip down. (Courtesy *The Western Horseman*)

time, then soaked it only twice during the second week. There was marked improvement in her gait by the second day of this treatment. Soon her walk was nearly normal and she even did some trotting and cantering, boot and all. After a couple weeks of wearing the boot, her foot had healed enough inside so that the mud and moisture could no longer enter the sensitive tissues, and I removed the boot for good.

Khamette was lucky that the puncture did not seriously damage any vital tissues of her foot. And because the wound was not treated immediately and the infection had to seek a drainage outlet, she was lucky the puncture was near the heel; the infection did not have far to go. In some cases permanent damage is done as the infection travels to find an outlet, following the line of least resistance and coming out near the heel. Khamette soon healed completely with no sign of lameness, but she would have healed much faster if I had been able to treat her properly sooner.

If you ever suspect a puncture wound in your horse, be sure to check the bottom of the foot thoroughly. A hoof tester can be very helpful in locating the area of soreness that should be probed.

A puncture wound in the foot should never be neglected. In some cases it may cause blood poisoning. Other conditions that can result from such a wound are infectious laminitis, or infection of the navicular bone or other important tissues of the foot.

7

SPLINTS: AN OUNCE OF PREVENTION IS WORTH A POUND OF CURE

We were both young. I was thirteen and in my first year of 4-H, and she was a three-year-old filly that I had trained—my first 4-H project. I didn't know about splints then, but I soon would, for it seems as though life teaches us most things by experience, the hard way.

My family's ranch was fourteen miles from town, and twice a week I rode Ginger the twenty-eight miles round trip to the county Fair Grounds where our 4-H horse club held its meetings and drill practices. On these trips Ginger and I traveled four miles on our hard-pack dirt road and the other ten miles along the shoulder of a highway. It would take us between one and a half and two and a half hours to travel the fourteen miles, walking and trotting, the length of time depending on how hot the day, how much trotting we did, and how much time we had in which to get there.

Being conscientious in what little I did know at that time, I never rode Ginger on the pavement, nor did I gallop her much, for I knew that faster gaits tire a horse unduly and I'd seen many of my young friends overdo the faster gaits, racing around like wild Indians with their horses in a lather. So Ginger and I developed a fast ground-covering trot. Indeed, she could trot so fast that other horses had to gallop to keep up. What I didn't know was that hard ground is almost as bad as pavement and that the shock of concussion is greater at the fast trot than at any other gait.

Ginger got "hard" that summer. I rode range on her as well as riding her to 4-H meetings. Some days we would even come home from town the long way through the hills and check on the range cattle, making our total trip easily forty miles or more.

But another thing I didn't know was that Ginger's conformation

82

Ginger as a six-year-old.

made her prone to splints from concussion. She was a chunky little horse with fairly upright shoulders and pasterns and a jarring gait, hence more concussion. By the spring she was four years old she had developed a splint on each front leg.

Splints are bony enlargements on the cannon bone. After I learned more about the structure of the horse's legs, I understood better the reasons why splints sometimes occur, and why Ginger developed them. An understanding of the horse's evolution helps explain the structure of the horse's legs.

The ancestor of the horse was the size of a small dog and had five toes. The first primitive horse had lost the two outermost toes and was a small animal with three toes on each foot. As evolution progressed, the two outer toes of these remaining three gradually became smaller until the horse was carrying his weight entirely on his enlarged middle toe. The outer toes eventually disappeared, but on the horse's legs today there are still vestiges of the bones that were attached to those toes. The horse's earliest ancestor originally had five of these metacarpal bones (front leg) and five metatarsal bones (hind leg). These five bones correspond to the bones in the human hand and foot.

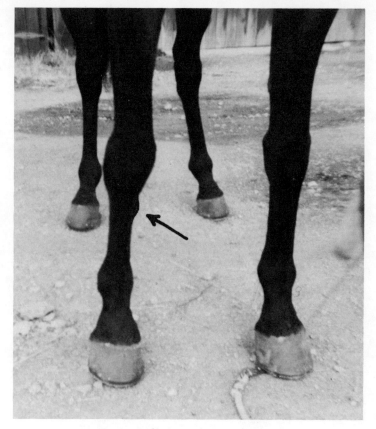

Arrow indicates splint on foreleg.

The outermost two or these five bones in the horse have completely disappeared, as have his outer two toes. The middle metacarpal (and metatarsal) has grown large and strong and is the cannon bone of the horse today. The second and fourth metacarpals are shortened and small and no longer serve any main purpose. They lie on each side of the cannon bone toward the rear and are called "splint bones."

Bones are covered with a thin layer of membrane called the periosteum, which nourishes and protects the bone. The periosteum also is important in bone growth, because it has a layer of special bone-forming cells. In young horses the splint bones are rather loosely attached to the cannon bone but become firmly attached by the time the horse is five or six years old. But sometimes, due to injury or vitamin deficiency or other disorders, the places where the splint bones attach to the cannon bone become inflamed and painful. Periostitis (inflammation of the periosteum) sets in whenever the periosteum is injured. Circulation

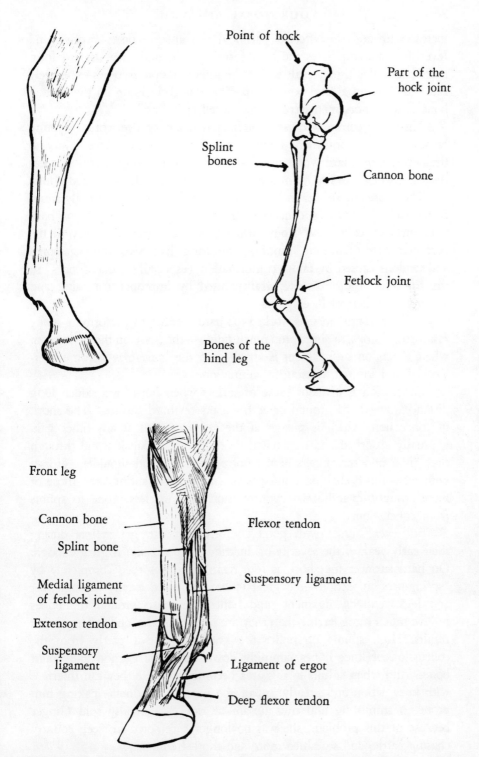

Point of hock

Part of the
hock joint

Splint
bones

Cannon bone

Fetlock joint

Bones of the
hind leg

Front leg

Cannon bone

Flexor tendon

Splint bone

Medial ligament
of fetlock joint

Suspensory ligament

Extensor tendon

Suspensory
ligament

Ligament of ergot

Deep flexor tendon

Hind leg of the horse (left), Bones of the Hind Leg (right), Front leg (bottom).

increases around the affected part and the area becomes swollen and feverish. This stimulates the bone-forming cells and they start to form more bone. The usual result is that the inflammation becomes excessively calcified, leaving a hard bony lump. This unsightly lump on the cannon bone is what horsemen have always called a "splint."

The most common cause of splints is strain or overwork in young horses, creating movement between the bones and therefore injury to the periosteum. Hard work often causes splints in young horses whereas the same work will not harm a mature horse with fully developed bones.

The causes of splints in horses under six years old are usually strain from fast stops or turns, concussion from trotting and galloping on hard road surfaces, concussion from jumping on hard ground, injury to the periosteum from slipping, running, or falling. Excessive strain on bones and tendons caused by faulty conformation (especially "bench knees" in the front legs) or excessive strain caused by improper trimming and shoeing can also produce splints.

When a young horse is worked too hard—either by performing many fast turns or stops, or simply too much riding—the place on the periosteum where a tendon or ligament is attached to the bone may become over-worked and injured, causing inflammation.

Concussion is a major cause of splints when horses are ridden long distances over hard ground or at fast gaits on hard surfaces. The shock of concussion, which is greater at the fast trot than at any other gait, is usually absorbed and distributed through foot expansion and through the "give" and springiness of the horse's pasterns and shoulders. Horses with well-sloped shoulders and pasterns have more spring than those of more straight-up-and-down conformation and are less prone to splints from concussion.

But even horses with good conformation can get splints during their early years if the severity or duration of concussion is great enough. On hard surfaces the shock is too great to be absorbed completely by "springiness" of action—too great to be distributed evenly through feet and legs, tendons, ligaments and bones. On hard ground the bones receive much more jarring than they are meant to take, and inflammation results. High splints up under the knee are caused partly from the concussion of knee bones jamming down upon the cannon and splint bones. And when splints in this area become too large they can interfere with knee action and greatly impair the horse's usefulness, making him prone to stumbling and thus unsafe to ride. We finally sold Ginger because of this problem; she was no longer surefooted in steep country chasing cattle, and stumbled more and more frequently.

A splint can also be caused by direct injury such as kick or a blow

A horse of good conformation with long sloping shoulders and long sloping pasterns has springier action and is less prone to splints.

A horse with poor conformation and short straight-up-and-down shoulders and pasterns has choppier action, a more jarring gait, and is more prone to splints from concussion.

or from running into something solid. Young horses can develop inflammation and potential splints from being bumped or kicked on the leg. Sometimes a horse of poor conformation will strike one leg with his other foot and cause injury that will produce a splint. Some young horses develop splints due to nutritional bone disease caused by inadequate or improper diet—vitamin deficiency, or excessive vitamin and mineral supplementation.

Splints can develop on any part of the splint bone. Each leg has two splint bones, eight altogether. But most splints occur on the inside of the front legs because these inner splint bones carry more weight than the outer ones and are therefore more subject to stress. Most splints appear about three inches below the knee.

Splints usually cause lameness only in the early stages. A few cases never cause lameness at all. When inflammation begins there might or might not be swelling with it, but careful examination of the lame leg will reveal the location of the soreness, for it will be hot, and painful to the horse when pressed. Lameness is most noticeable at the trot and most severe after the horse has been ridden or exercised on hard ground. In mild cases there will be no lameness evident at the walk.

In time the splint calcifies and the hard permanent lump develops.

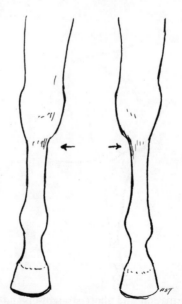

Offset, or "Bench" knees. The cannon bones are set too far to the outside, giving the horse a bow-legged appearance. The inner splint bone (inside of the foreleg) is under greater stress than in a horse of normal conformation and splints are common.

Lameness usually disappears and the splint is then considered a blemish rather than an unsoundness. The exceptions are splints caused by poor conformation (such as "bench knees," or by a poor way of traveling and striking the leg with the other foot, etc.) or cases where the splint interferes with a moving part: a high splint hindering action of the knee joint, or a "pegged splint" which goes around the back of the leg interfering with the ligaments and tendons. Most splints are merely blemishes, but an old splint can flare up and become a problem if it is struck or reinjured.

Splints are almost impossible to remove once they have calcified (except by surgery, and even then the bony growth returns in about half of the cases), so it is important to diagnose them early. Old chronic splints are best left alone, though sometimes pegged splints can be surgically removed if they vitally hinder the usefulness of a valuable horse.

If a young (and by young I mean any horse under seven years old) horse you are riding turns up lame, strain or concussion may well be the cause if no other condition is obvious. Fracture of the splint bone is often confused with splints, but with a fractured splint bone the swelling of the limb is usually spread over a larger area and the horse remains lame for a longer period. If you ever suspect that one of the splint bones may be broken you should have a vet check the horse and X-ray the limb. A fractured splint can be a serious problem and some of the treatments used for ordinary splints will only make the fracture worse.

The best treatment for a potential splint caused by strain or concussion is *rest*. Do not use the horse at all. Pasture rest is ideal and much better for the horse than being kept in a stall.

Treatment for early periostitis is anti-inflammatory, using cold packs and astringents and anti-inflammatory drugs. Resting the horse for at least thirty days or longer while continuing treatment will often be sufficient for the splint to heal.

Treatment for a splint that is already producing new bone growth (chronic splint) is more complicated, and effectiveness of the treatment varies. Veterinarians use several methods of treatment. Some use firing, or cauterize the splint deeply, or inject cortisone directly into the inflamed area. Some use counterirritants such as blistering. However, once the new bone growth has started, it is not always possible to prevent the calcifying process that results in a disfiguring splint.

Needless to say, prevention is all-important. Do not start riding young horses too soon, and don't progress too fast with strenuous work or training until they are mature. A good horseman thinks first of his horse, and takes his *time*. In training a young horse there are more important goals than being able to compete in the next horse show or trail ride.

Another good rule to remember: never trot or gallop a horse on pavement, gravel, or hard ground. This goes for horses of all ages, for there are other ailments besides splints that can be caused by concussion, including founder, sidebones, and navicular disease.

If you ride your horse wisely you will probably not have to worry about the problem of splints.

8

HORSESHOEING

"What will we do now?" we asked each other. Our horses quickened their walk, heading toward home. My younger brother wiped the sweat from his forehead and glanced down at his mare's right front foot. She wasn't limping much, yet. It had been a long hot day. What had begun early that morning as a routine ride to check range cattle had taken till late afternoon because we had found some cattle down on Dry Flat and had moved them back up Baker Creek to better grass. In the process Ginger had lost a shoe. We hadn't noticed she'd lost it until our cattle-driving was done and we were starting on our way home.

Ordinarily the loss of a shoe wouldn't have been a crisis. Dad could have reshod Ginger's foot for us when we got home. My brother Rocky and I would be making another long ride the next day, riding Nell and Ginger the twenty-eight-mile round trip to town for our 4-H meeting and drill practice. Rocky and I were twelve and fourteen years old, and Nell and Ginger were our 4-H projects.

But this week our parents and baby sister Heidi were away on a trip and we were there at the ranch "holding the fort" alone. We'd been busy—doing the irrigating and the range riding, and we even fixed a bad spot in the fence where one of the neighbor's cows had gotten in. But tomorrow was the day we would ride to town, and here was Ginger without a shoe. She'd never make it; already the rocks were making her foot tender.

Maybe we could put a shoe on her ourselves. . . . The thought was a brave one, but not impossible, for I'd trimmed some of our horses' feet and had removed shoes. I'd watched Dad shoe our horses many times, but I had never attempted the job myself.

So when we got home we found the shoeing tools and one of Ginger's used shoes from last year. It looked as if it still had enough "wear" left in it to last as long as the rest of the set she was wearing.

The only thing that worried me was that I couldn't think which way the nails went; whether it was the rough side or the smooth side of the head that faced inward. All we could do was go ahead and find out. I leveled the foot as best I could, placed the shoe as straight as I could, then began cautiously driving the first nail, asking Rocky (who was overseeing the job) with every hammer tap whether the nail tip had started to show through the hoof wall yet. When I had driven it halfway in and the tip still hadn't started to come through, I decided I must have the nail in wrong and pulled it out. I placed the second nail the other way, and when it came through properly we knew we were on the right track. Thus I learned, and never again forgot, the little rule for horseshoe nails: "rough side inside." We got the shoe on, and must have clinched it well enough, for it stayed on all through the next day's long ride (though I watched Ginger's foot apprehensively nearly all the way!) and didn't come off until we took the whole set off to be replaced a month later.

Because this first attempt was a success, I saw no reason why I shouldn't do more shoeing, even though I was a girl and only fourteen. Dad didn't mind; shoeing bothered his back. I gradually took over the job of shoeing all our horses—Nell, Ginger, old Possum, big Nosey

Trimming Nosey's feet. (Nosey was our old pack horse.)

Shoeing Nikki

the pack horse, Scrappy, and then my own Khamette when she grew up. As I became more proficient, I shod a few horses for friends and neighbors as well.

After Lynn and I were married I shod his mare for him the first year. But then, not to be outdone, he took up horseshoeing too and has become quite good at it. Now we often team up when one of our horses needs to be shod, and get the job done in almost half the time. One of us can trim and level a foot while the other shapes a shoe, and so forth. And it's good to be able to take a breather between shoes while the other person takes over for a while. The job certainly goes faster. So far we haven't tried working on two feet at once, but I've heard it can be done!

We've found it convenient to be able to shoe our own horses, and you might also. There are many advantages. We save the cost of hiring a farrier. Perhaps even more important than cost is time: when a horse needs foot care we can give it immediately without having to make an appointment or wait for a farrier. Time is important on our ranch when we use our horses so much. And we know our own horses well. We have seen them in action hundreds of times, we know how they handle their feet, how their feet wear and how they grow—so we are able to trim and shoe them properly. Besides, our horses know us and are used to being handled by us. The young horses we raise are easy

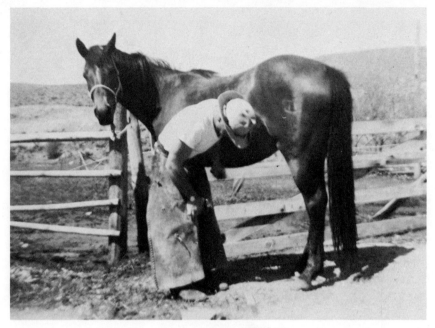

Lynn shoeing Nikki.

to shoe for the first time because they are accustomed to our handling.

Shoeing is a "necessary evil" in our part of the country because of the rocky terrain. The horse evolved and developed on grassy plains where he did not need shoes. But here the rocks and the steady riding wear down their hoofs much faster than they grow.

"No foot, no horse" is an old saying that is certainly true as far as the working ability of the horse is concerned. Care of the horse's feet is one of the most important aspects of taking care of the horse. A horse's feet deteriorate when he is not used or exercised. A horse is as old as his feet and legs, for if they go bad he is useless.

Thousands of years ago people devised ways to protect the hoofs of the horses they rode, using everything from socks to sandals. But the practice of nailing iron shoes to the hoof was not introduced until the second century B.C. and was not commonly known until the end of the fifth century A.D. Shoeing as we know it today was not in regular use until the Middle Ages.

Horses are individuals. Each one is built a little differently, and the feet of each horse have a different shape and hardness and rate of hoof growth. Moist climates tend to make a hoof softer. The Arabian horse of the desert and the mustang of the American West and other horses developing in similar environments have the toughest hoofs. There are great differences among our own horses. Nell, Nikki, and Fahleen have good, well-formed feet, but they become tender very quickly when they go barefoot on our rocky terrain. Scrappy and her Half-Arabian daughter Khamette have feet so hard and tough that they are hard to trim. Scrappy is of mixed breeding that includes some unknown and some "mustang" blood and she can be ridden part of the summer before she needs shoes, whereas most of our other horses need shoes right from the start. Bambi and Ginger each have one white foot. These non-pigmented hoofs are softer and more easily broken and worn down. And because they are softer they do not always hold a shoe as well. This is why we don't like stocking feet on a horse.

The outside horny shell of the hoof is a protective covering for the sensitive tissues inside—bones, nerves, blood vessels, tendons, etc. Nature has provided a unique covering that grows continually to compensate for the wear and tear of traveling. This outside covering consists of the hoof wall, the sole of the foot, the frog, and the bars. The V-shaped frog serves as a cushion, helps absorb concussion, and helps regulate the moisture of the hoof. The hoof wall carries most of the horse's weight and the bars serve as a brace to prevent overexpansion and contraction of the foot. The sole is concave to give grip and to allow for expansion. If any of these outer tissues are abused by injury or by excessive trimming, the normal functions and soundness of the entire hoof are at stake.

Front hoofs are usually larger, rounder, and stronger than hind ones because the front feet support nearly two-thirds of the horse's weight. Most horses need front shoes slightly larger than their hind shoes.

The hoof wall grows downward from the coronary band just under the hairline at the top of the hoof. Any injury to the coronary band will

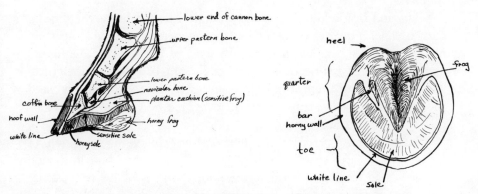

Cross section of the foot (left), Parts of the foot (right).

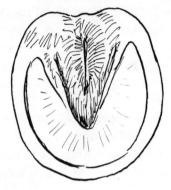

Front hoofs (left) are larger and rounder than hind hoofs (right). Hind hoofs are more pointed.

affect the growth of the hoof. The average rate of hoof growth is about one-fourth to three-eighths of an inch per month, and the entire hoof wall is usually replaced by new horn every eight to ten months.

The horny sole grows downward from the sensitive inner sole. As it continues to grow, little cracks develop in the old sole, for the outer layer is dead tissue. Nature has provided that these parts of the foot will "trim" themselves. This process is called exfoliation, or a flaking off of dead tissue. A horse's sole usually does not need to be trimmed much. Occasionally loose dead tissue builds up, and this should be peeled away with the hoof knife, or this layer of dead tissue will provide a place for the generation of bacteria and hoof diseases.

In unshod horses the bottom of the hoof wall, the frog and the bars of the foot are all level and flat to the ground and each helps bear the weight of the horse. The bars are very important because they act as a wedge to keep the heels from caving in and contracting. The bars should never be trimmed excessively or cut away when the hoof is trimmed.

Bars and frog seldom strike the ground in a shod horse, for shoeing puts the hoof a quarter of an inch or more above the ground, by-passing nature's plan for bars and frog to take some of the weight. The horse's ancestors roamed prairie country and could run barefoot all their lives without becoming "tender-footed," but horses in rocky country need shoes to keep from wearing down their feet too fast and to avoid lameness from stone bruises.

Before starting to trim the horse's feet, observe the position of his legs when he is standing squarely, and then observe him in motion (at walk and trot) to determine the normal angles of his feet. Notice the point at which the foot breaks over or leaves the ground, and any deviations in gait. Uneven wear of the foot shows that the animal is not traveling straight. A horse that travels straight on sound feet and legs will wear the hoof (or the shoe) evenly, with slightly more wear at the center of the toe.

When the horse is standing squarely there should be about a 45-degree angle in the slope of the pastern. Individual horses will vary somewhat from this; some have more sloping pasterns, others more upright. The ideal angle is around 45 degrees for the front pasterns. Hind pasterns tend to be a little more upright; 55 degrees is the normal angle here.

However, trimming should not be too drastic in an effort to give the horse's feet a perfect angle, because each horse has his own angle and any radical changes can cause problems. The foot should be trimmed so that the pastern and hoof are on the same angle, forming an unbroken line, whatever that angle may be for that particular horse. If the toes are too long, this angle line will be broken, throwing a strain on the legs and eventually causing unsoundness. If the heel and hind parts of the hoof are too long, the line will be broken in the other direction. You will have to judge how much hoof to take off to make the foot level at the proper angle.

Hold a front foot securely between your knees as you clean and trim the hoof in preparation for the shoe. A hind foot is held across the thigh.

The first step is cleaning all dirt and debris from the hoof with a hoof pick. Then remove the dead tissue of the sole with a hoof knife. All loose material should be scraped away, but do not trim much deeper, for the horse needs this protection for the inner structures of

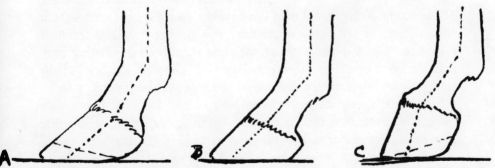

A. Toe is too long and should be trimmed to bring foot to the proper angle.

B. Normal foot—angle unbroken.

C. Heel and quarters too long, breaking the angle of the foot.

his foot. After the frog is trimmed of loose tags the extra growth of the outer hoof wall can be trimmed level with the sole (except at the quarters) with hoof cutters. The hoof cutters should be held in such a way that they make a flat, level cut. Trimming should be done from heel to toe or in a complete circle from heel to heel. In order to make a flat surface, you will have to leave a little extra wall at the quarters (because the sole at the quarters is concave); if you cut this area level with the sole you will have cut away too much and the wall will not meet the shoe here. The bars should be trimmed level with the wall at the heels.

Then the hoof wall is rasped smooth to make a level seat for the shoe. The rasp should be held flat and level so that one side of the wall is not made lower than the other.

If the horse is to go barefoot, you should leave about a quarter of an inch of hoof wall projecting below the sole when you trim the foot. And the outside edges of the wall should be smoothed and rounded with the rasp; leaving a sharp outside edge increases the chance of splitting or cracking or chipping away of the wall. If you are shoeing the horse, trim the wall level with the sole at the toe, and as low as necessary at the heel to establish the proper foot angle.

The shoe should be shaped to fit the hoof, and should fit evenly—the bottom of the hoof wall should rest flat against the shoe. The heels of the shoe should not stick out behind the heel of the foot, especially on the front feet or the horse may step on his front shoes with his hind feet, yet the heels of the shoe must be well under the horse's heels. The heels of the hoof must rest on the shoe in order to permit proper hoof expansion and contraction. If the shoe is too short, or it does not properly fit at the quarters and heel, the shoe may cut into the foot as the hoof wall grows or cause corns or other problems that can produce lameness. The branches of the shoe should extend wider than the hoof wall—about one-sixteenth of an inch—at the heel and quarter to allow for hoof expansion. The last nail hole of the shoe should not be farther back than the bend of the quarter. If the last nail is beyond the bend of the hoof wall at the quarter, expansion of the hoof will be limited.

The shoe should be centered properly on the foot. For horses with normal feet, the shoe can be centered by using the point of the frog as a guide. But in horses that toe in or out, the frog usually points off center and the shoe cannot be centered this way. If a hoof is worn excessively on one side because of poor conformation or if part of the hoof wall has been broken away, it might not be possible to make the foot level by trimming, without trimming *too* much on the opposite side. The branch of the shoe on the worn side can be shimmed with leather so that the foot will be level when the shoe is on.

When the shoe has been properly shaped to fit the foot, the nails can be driven in. The nails should have heads that protrude a little after they are driven in; a nail that fits too deeply into the crease, with a nail head too small, will not hold as well and the shoe may become loose.

The nail should enter the hoof at the white line. In nailing the shoe on, hold the nail with thumb and index finger. The shoe can be held in the proper position by your hand resting on it as you hold the nail. Location of the first nail to be driven does not matter a great deal as long as the shoe is properly centered and is not out of position after the nail is driven. After the first two nails are driven, one on each side of the shoe, the shoe will stay in place without being held as you drive the rest of the nails.

The beveled side of the nail point should be toward the inside so that the nail will be directed outward as it is driven. The beveled side can be determined by the rough side of the nail head; they are both on the inside of the nail. The nail should be held straight and "aimed" for the spot where it should come out on the hoof wall. The nail should come out about three-quarters inch above the shoe or about a third of the way up the wall. The actual distance will depend of course on how large the horse is—a draft horse will have much bigger feet than an Arabian, for instance, larger nails will be used, and the nails

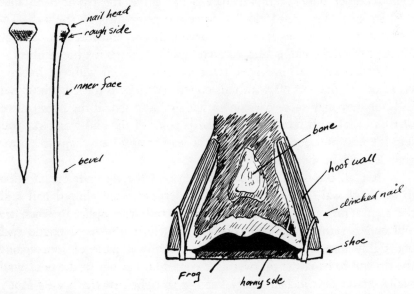

Horseshoe nail and Cross Section of Shod Hoof. Shoe should stick out a little past the hoof wall at the quarters to allow for foot expansion.

will come out higher in the hoof wall. If a nail comes out much too high or too low, it should be pulled and redriven. Nails driven to a uniform height give the shod foot a good appearance, but if the nail comes out somewhere near the desired position, it is best to let it stay there. If it is pulled and redriven to make a better appearance, the second perforation may weaken the hoof wall and eventually cause a loose shoe.

The driven nails should go into the outer portion of the hoof wall. They should never be driven inside of the white line that separates the wall from the sole, or they will go into the sensitive part of the hoof. The nails must be placed correctly (rough side inside) before being driven so that they will curve outward and come out the side of the hoof wall instead of curving into the sensitive part of the foot. And the nails should not be driven too straight (especially on a horse with small feet) or they may come out too high; a "high" nail is more apt to prick or put pressure, if it bends much inside, on the sensitive tissues.

If the horse flinches greatly during the driving of a nail, the sensitive tissues may have been pricked or punctured. In this case the nail should be pulled and iodine should be applied to the nail hole.

If light taps of the hammer are used, the point of the nail will travel parallel with the fibers of the hoof wall and will not sever these fibers. To drive the nail through the outer wall at the desired place, use light hammer blows until the nail is two-thirds the required distance, then strike a sharp, hard blow to force the point through the wall. The bevel on the point makes the nail curve outward, and this bevel is most effective when the nail is being driven rapidly through the horny fibers.

As soon as a nail is driven, twist the end of it off with the hammer claws or cut the end off with nail cutters (and keep track of those nail ends, or they may cause someone a flat tire!) so that if the horse moves or tries to take his foot away, the sharp point of the nail won't cut your leg. It's always a good idea to wear a leather apron or chaps to protect your legs while shoeing.

After all the nails have been driven and the tip ends cut off close to the hoof wall, cut a small notch underneath each clipped nail with the rasp. This notch will keep the hoof wall from splitting when the nail end is turned over and clinched. To clinch the nails, pound each one tighly into the shoe crease while holding a piece of iron against the tip end to bend the tip over as it comes farther out of the hoof wall. Nails should be clinched firmly but not so tight that the horse's foot is made sore and "nail bound." Finish bending the nails with the hammer, pounding the tips flat down against the hoof wall (into the notch you

Leveling the foot for the shoe, with the rasp.

Setting the first nail.

Driving the nails.

Twisting off the driven nail tip with the hammer claws.

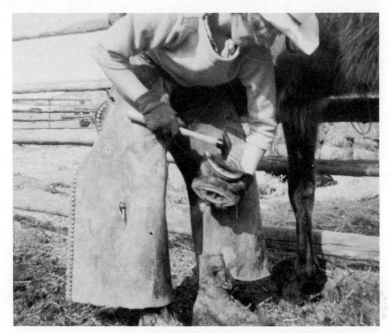

Clinching the nails.

cut) to finish the clinch. A short clinch holds better than a long one, as well as looking neater. A long clinch is more apt to be knocked and unbent in rocks and will work loose faster.

With the rasp you can smooth the outside edge of the hoof where it meets the shoe, but be careful not to rasp the hoof wall too much. This horny wall is made up of tiny tubes and excessive rasping cuts these tubes and leaves them open, allowing the hoof to dry out. If the shoe was properly fitted and nailed with no slipping, little or no rasping will be needed on the outside of the hoof wall to smooth it to the shoe.

When you are removing a shoe (removing shoes for the winter or removing shoes to trim the feet and reset the shoes), cut the clinched nails on the hoof wall with a clinch cutter. Then pick up the foot and use pulling pincers (or else old hoof nippers can be used if you have no pulling pincers). The pincers should be placed under the shoe, starting at the heel. Then close the handle and push outward, slightly toward the middle line of the foot. After that heel branch is loosened, the opposite heel should be loosened. Hold the foot securely and never twist the pincers or pull crookedly, and you will not injure the horse. Continue working down both of the branches until the entire shoe is loosened. After you have removed the shoe, pull any pieces of nail that might be left in the hoof wall, and then proceed to trim the foot. Feet should be trimmed, or shoes reset, every four to six weeks, depending on the individual horse's rate of hoof growth, and the amount of wear on the feet if he is barefoot. A barefoot horse that gets some wear on his feet may not need to be trimmed this often.

To keep your horse's feet healthy, they should be kept properly trimmed, and properly shod when he must travel through rocky terrain. The horse should never be kept in a muddy corral or swampy pasture; if his feet are always packed with muck he will be prone to foot diseases such as thrush. Clean his feet before each ride to remove packed dirt or any rocks he may have picked up. A rock carried in the horse's foot may bruise the sole or frog or heel and make him lame for some time.

Clean the hoof with a hoof pick or some other suitable tool. Never use a sharp instrument that might cut or puncture if you slipped or if the horse happened to jerk his foot. Handle your horse's feet often enough so that you are able to recognize any unnatural heat or swelling in the foot or leg. Don't neglect cracks, chipped hoofs, or lameness; take care of them as soon as you notice them in order to keep them from becoming worse.

If the horse is going to be turned out to pasture for quite a while without use, pull his shoes so that his frog, bars, and heels can function normally. But if the pasture is rocky, or if the horse is wintering out in rocky country, you may want to keep him shod. Just be sure that his shoes are reset or replaced periodically even if you aren't using him, or his feet will grow too long and put strain on his bones and tendons. Nature did not intend the horse to wear shoes, but in many places shoes are a necessary evil, and a proper job of shoeing will not hinder the horse. Well-fitting shoes will enable him to travel comfortably.

Here are some general rules to keep in mind when shoeing a horse:

1. Shoes should be as light as possible, taking into consideration the wear demanded of them, to interfere as little as possible with the normal flight of the horse's foot.
2. The ground surface should be plain. A plain plate shoe will hinder the horse least and interfere least with his way of going. Toe and heel calks are not advisable except for draft horses or for ice, or for other special conditions where a certain amount and kind of extra traction is needed. We sometimes use calks on our horses in the mountains.
3. Nails should take a short, thick hold on the hoof wall. They should not be too high. Thus the old nail holes can be removed with the natural growth of the hoof the next time the horse is shod. This is especially important if the horse is used much and will be wearing out his shoes frequently, as when he is used

riding range, or in training for competitive endurance and trail rides, etc. If the horse must be shod often, you will want room in the hoof for the new nails for such succeeding set of shoes.

Now let's look at the importance of proper foot care in the foal and growing young horse. If neglected, a foal with good legs and feet can become crooked-legged, pigeon-toed, or splay-footed. While the young horse is still growing, tendons, ligaments and even bones are pliable; a crooked leg can be straightened or a good leg damaged, depending on proper care and attention or the lack of it. The foal's feet should be trimmed regularly and properly, never taking off too much horn at any one time (remember that in the foal's tiny feet the slightest amount of unevenness or irregularity will be a lot) and being careful to trim the foot as level as possible. When a foal has crooked legs, trim the foot to slightly unbalance the foot in the proper direction to straighten the leg. This should always be done gradually; overzealous corrective trimming will only put a strain on the legs, so never make an abrupt change. The younger the horse, the better your chances of making permanent improvements in a crooked leg. Corrective trimming is best done in gradual stages between three and eighteen months of age. If you have never done any corrective trimming before, it would be wise to have a farrier trim the foal's feet. He may be able to explain the procedures necessary to straighten the legs so that you can trim him yourself the next time, but if you are unsure of yourself it is best to let an experienced shoer trim that foal—you sure don't want him to grow up with poor feet and legs!

We keep a foot-care chart on all our horses. You might find it a worthwhile idea, too. The main purpose of this chart is to help us trim and shoe our horses regularly, never letting their feet grow too long. You can easily tell by looking at a horse's feet whether or not his feet are growing too long, but it is handy and helpful to keep accurate dates on trimming and shoeing, especially if a person has several horses; the chart and its dates are a good reminder when it's time to trim feet or reset a horse's shoes, especially during times of the year that you might not be seeing the horse often to look at his feet (as when he is on winter pasture).

The foot-care chart we use is one we've adapted from the system used in the 4-H horse club I belonged to when I was young, a system devised by our 4-H leader, Mrs. Jerry Ravndal. A round symbol ○ represents the horse—as if you were looking down at him from above his back, as though you were riding him. Four lines represent his four feet. A line is drawn whenever that foot is shod. Thus, a circle with only one line in the right front leg position would mean the horse was shod on the right front foot; the number within the circle represents the day of the month. Lines representing hind legs show when the hind feet were shod, etc. A simple circle means that the horse's feet were trimmed. We usually make a few explanatory notes on the chart at times, to indicate if a shoe is lost, whether shoes were replaced or reset, or to indicate any corrective trimming or shoeing procedures, etc. This system is quick and easy, taking up very little space, and is also very easy to read. Try it!

9

CARE OF THE FOALING MARE

The birth of a foal is an exciting event that is eagerly awaited, and an event which should be carefully prepared for. You've been waiting approximately eleven months for the new arrival and you will want to be sure that everything goes well.

The time to start proper care of the brood mare is before she is even bred. The importance of adequate care and proper feeding cannot be overemphasized. The horse has the lowest conception rate and the highest mortality rate among newborns of any domestic animal, but many of these misses or fatalities can be prevented by proper care.

The mare should be in good physical condition before she is bred. She should not be too thin or too fat. Mares that are thin and under-nourished may not even come in heat. Mares that are too fat are hard to settle. A thin mare in a "gaining" condition will actually settle more easily than an overly fat mare.

She should be fed a high protein hay or be on good pasture. Some mares will need some supplementary grain even with good hay or pasture; others won't. If your pasture is poor or growing on poor land, or if you are feeding poor quality hay, you must feed a larger grain supplement. Additional mineral and vitamin supplement may be necessary, too, unless your pasture or hay is top quality and not grown in deficient or depleted soils.

It's a good idea to worm the mare. You'll want everything in her favor when she is carrying her foal so that it will be a healthy one; you don't want internal parasites to rob the mare of proper nutrition and vitality. Also, you should have her checked thoroughly by a vet for breeding soundness. This can save you time and money by locating potential trouble and correcting it before it interferes with conception or endangers the unborn foal.

Newborn foal napping in the sunshine.

A mare should not be bred until she is mature and full grown; breeding a filly too young will stunt her growth and be hard on her. Some horses mature faster than others and can be bred at three, to foal at four. But as a general rule, we feel a mare should not be bred until she is four, to foal at five.

When breeding the mare, you will want to consider heredity and conformation. You may not possess the perfect or ideal mare, but you can always try to select the best available sire, one that has the qualities you are looking for in the foal, and preferably a sire that is strong in areas where your mare may be weak. For instance, if your mare has a poor head, or poor neck, or poor croup, etc., you'd want to choose a stallion that had excellent conformation in the area your mare is lacking, on the chance that the foal might inherit the better quality from the stallion.

Above all, when considering conformation, look for a stallion with very good feet and legs, good straight action, etc. Whether you plan to use the foal as a pleasure horse, show horse, stock horse, race horse, or trail horse, he will be more successful and worth more to you if he has good sound legs and a smooth, straight way of going. He will be better able to perform in whatever role you place him. Action and conformation are extremely important and make the difference between a good horse and a poor one. But don't forget disposition. This is a heritable factor also. You'd rather raise a foal with a friendly, intelligent disposition than one with a cranky and belligerent temperament.

A mare can be bred any time of year if she is healthy and her estrus cycle is regular, but there are many advantages to breeding in the spring. In the spring the mare is on green grass and the warmer weather and lengthening days will make her come in heat more readily and settle easier. The foal will be born the next spring during good weather (you won't want your mare foaling in cold or foul weather unless you have the proper facilities to shelter her) and he will have green pasture during the months he will be growing the fastest.

Egg release in the mare, called ovulation, is not completely automatic. Outside factors, such as the season of the year, the mare's general health, social stimulation by other horses, and so forth, seem to affect it. Light seems to be a factor. The lengthening days of April, May, and June are the best times to breed a mare. Also, nature regards breeding as somewhat of a luxury and won't allow it unless the mare is in good health. The social aspect is not to be ignored either. The ovulation process is helped when a mare can see a stallion or other horses from time to time. Loneliness seems to hinder normal ovulation.

The mare usually comes in heat every fourteen to twenty-one days if she is not pregnant. The heat period in mares is relatively long (three to seven days) compared with that of other farm animals. When a mare comes in heat she may be restless, or she may play up to the other horses in the pasture or across the fence, or be more cranky and quarrelsome than usual. Sometimes she will urinate frequently, or there may be a discharge from the vagina. Mares vary in how they act when in heat.

It is a good idea to leave the mare at the stud farm for a while so that when she does come in heat she can be bred at the proper time. The mare will be more apt to come into heat properly and conceive if she has a chance to get accustomed to the strange surroundings, strange feed and water, and acquainted with the stallion *before* she comes in heat. Sudden changes can often be upsetting to a mare and throw her off schedule.

For successful breeding, timing is important. Ovulation takes place about twenty-four to forty-eight hours before the end of heat. Because mares vary in the length of their heat periods, they are usually bred the second or third day of heat, and every other day thereafter as long as the heat period lasts.

During the time the mare is carrying her foal, she should have the best care possible. She should be kept in good condition, but not overfed. As I mentioned in the chapter on feeding, a pregnant mare's feed requirements increase significantly only during the last part of her pregnancy. Many horsemen start feeding a mare extra as soon as she becomes pregnant; as a result they have a mare that is too fat when her time comes to foal. The proper amount of feed is important. Perhaps even more important is the *quality* of the feed. Huge amounts of feed won't do the mare any good if it lacks the proper nutrition she needs.

Exercise is very important. The mare's muscles should be in good condition, not soft and flabby from nonuse. A mare that is too fat or out of condition will have more trouble giving birth to her foal. *Muscles* are required to expel the foal in the act of labor, so good muscle tone is important. Some horsemen make the mistake of allowing a brood mare little or no exercise for fear of hurting her or the unborn foal. But the pregnant mare is *not* a fragile creature, and she should have exercise.

A large pasture where she can move around freely can provide the needed exercise. If you have no pasture and she must be kept in a stall or corral, ride her or lead her for an hour or more every day. If you have been riding her before she was bred, by all means keep riding her after she is pregnant. Just use good judgment in how you ride her. She should not be ridden fast or hard in steep or rough country, nor required to make sudden starts, stops, or quick turns at high speeds. Don't use her for jumping. As she gets heavy with foal, avoid prolonged downhill riding; the weight of the unborn foal can put pressure on her heart and lungs and make her very uncomfortable. But sensible, moderate riding will do her good.

When the mare is pregnant keep her with just a few horses she gets along with, preferably a few other mares. Young horses, geldings, or a large number of any type of horses increase the chances of injury to the mare or unborn foal from being kicked or from slipping and falling while running. You can keep the mare by herself if she has companionship over the fence with other horses. Sometimes even just a goat or a cow will provide her all the company she needs. You should remove as many obstacles as possible from the area in which you keep the mare. Avoid narrow gates and doorways. Don't let the horses crowd through a gate in groups. In the stall, remove all projecting edges that the mare might run into.

The quality and development of a foal depends somewhat on the care of the mare before foaling. If she is undernourished, rundown, or has a deficiency of vitamins or minerals, the foal may be underdeveloped or may not even survive.

If you live in an iodine-deficient area, you should give the mare supplementary iodine (iodized salt will take care of this). Your veterinarian can tell you whether or not it is necessary to supplement in your area. Lack of iodine can cause contracted tendons in the foal. In our part of the country our hay is a little short of vitamin A. Ask your vet about giving your mare shots of vitamins A and D, and perhaps a little supplementary calcium.

There are some diseases that must be guarded against when preparing for the new foal. One of the worst of these is called "navel ill" or "joint ill." The bacteria that cause it live in the ground and enter the newborn foal through the navel after the umbilical cord has ruptured following birth. Once the bacteria are present in the soil in a certain area, they will always be there.

Even if you think your area might be free from joint ill, it is always a good idea to vaccinate against it. You should have the vaccine on hand well ahead of the time your mare is due to foal, in case the foal comes early. A mixed equine vaccine is sometimes used, as it protects the foal from several other diseases as well as joint ill. Check with your veterinarian.

Some horsemen prefer to vaccinate the mare before she foals, to start building up an immunity in the foal. In rare cases the mare herself is a carrier of joint ill and her foal will be born with the disease already in progress. This happens when the mare has a low-grade uterine infection that was not properly cleared up before she was bred. If a foal is

The foal can be held or "led" by using one arm around his hindquarters and one around his chest. This is a good way to "lead" him when moving him from one place to another, and a good way to hold him when he is being given a shot.

born with the disease already in progress, antibiotics must be given immediately to save the foal and to prevent crippling of the joints. If you decide to vaccinate the mare, do it about three weeks before she is due to foal. Five cc. is the proper dosage.

After the foal arrives, it should be vaccinated immediately with 5 cc. whether or not the mare was vaccinated. The foal should be given a second vaccination a week after the first one. Use a small horse needle on the foal. To avoid giving him a sore neck (which might interfere with his nursing), vaccinate him in the large muscle below the buttocks. When giving shots, make sure your equipment is sterilized, and avoid hitting a bone. The foal can be easily held with one arm around his chest and the other around his hindquarters (it helps to back him into a corner or have him against the stall wall or corral fence) while another person gives the shot.

Before the mare's foaling time approaches, you should give some thought as to where she will foal. If she must foal in a small enclosure, shed or box stall, it must first be thoroughly cleaned and then provided with clean bedding. The best place for a healthy mare with a history of normal and easy deliveries is a level, grassy pasture where she can be by herself. It should be a clean, dry place, with safe and smooth fencing. It should not have rough underbrush, gullies or other hazards— no loose wire, nails sticking out, machinery and the like, that might injure her or the foal. And there should be no water puddles, swampy areas, or ditches. Foals have been known to drown in even a tiny pool of water before they had a chance to get up. Even a dry ditch can cause trouble if the foal happens to roll into it. A foal cannot stay on its back safely for very long; abdominal pressure begins to cramp the heart and lungs and in a short time it will suffocate. Some owners have lost foals that got down on their backs in a dry ditch or under a fence.

But there are several advantages to having the mare foal out in a pasture. It is more natural for her to seek her own private place in the out-of-doors, and she will be less upset and nervous. Another advantage is the fact that there are fewer chances of infection in a grassy pasture than in a stall or corral. The problem of infection is always present when livestock are kept in confined areas. But there are disadvantages to pasture foaling as well. It is harder to keep close watch on the mare. Most breeders like to keep close track of a mare when she foals, especially a mare that has never had a foal before and might need help. And pasture foaling is not ideal in extremely wet or cold weather.

Most horses do not need help when foaling and are better off without it, but most horsemen don't like to take even the slightest chance of losing a foal in case something *does* go wrong. Some breeders let a mare out in a clean, safe pasture during the day and put her in a clean stall at night where she will be easier to check on.

If you keep the mare in a stall when she foals, you must first thoroughly clean and then disinfect the stall. The stall should be large enough to give the mare plenty of room to move around, for when she goes into labor she will be very restless. A box stall sixteen feet by sixteen feet is suitable. The stall should be built in such a way that you will be able to check on the mare's progress without disturbing her, without her seeing you.

Clean out any old bedding from the stall and then carefully scrub the whole stall with disinfectants, floor, walls, and all. Sprinkle the floor with slaked lime before putting in new bedding. Clean, bright straw makes good bedding; don't use any that is old and dusty or moldy. Cover the stall floor deep enough to be comfortable to the mare, but don't have the straw so deep that it will be hard for the new foal to get up and walk around. Sawdust or shavings should not be used for bedding because these can be sucked into the newborn foal's nostrils and lungs, and also will stick to the newborn foal and create a problem when the mare tries to lick him dry. Remove all obstacles from the stall, feed tubs, buckets, or anything else that might get in the mare's way during her act of labor.

About 336 days from the time the mare was bred, the foal should arrive. This gestation length, however, is just an average; not many mares foal precisely on the day they are supposed to. The period of gestation may vary greatly; mares have been known to foal as early as the 287th and as late as the 419th day. The light breeds (saddle horses) tend to have a longer gestation period than draft breeds. Gestation periods ending in fall and summer are usually shorter than those ending in spring or winter. This fact has been borne out by our own mares. Nell, for instance, had three summer foals (two colts and a filly) anywhere from one to two weeks early, and one early spring foal (a filly, in early March) several days late. Why mares carry their foals longer in winter and early spring is not clear, but it may be due to the greater intensity of the sun's rays in summer and fall, longer daylight hours, or better nutrition during certain phases of the gestation period, bringing a summer foal to full term sooner.

Watch the mare carefully as her foaling time approaches. Some mares will foal a few days early, some a few days late, depending on the individual mare and also upon the season of the year, as previously mentioned. Two or three weeks early or late is not uncommon, but if your mare goes more than two weeks past her foaling date you should have a vet check her to make sure nothing is wrong.

As foaling time approaches, the mare's udder fills and begins to look shiny. There may be a secretion from the teats. This "waxing" from the teats is one of the most common signs that foaling is near. The "wax" is formed by the congealing of secretions from the udder that are forced out the end of the teat. Most mares will wax profusely within twenty-four to thirty-six hours of the beginning of labor, but there are always individual differences. Some mares don't wax much at all. A few will wax for a week or ten days. Still others may make a great deal of mammary development and leak streams of milk before they foal. The mare may leak milk for just a few hours or for several days before she foals.

When you suspect her foaling time is near, put her by herself. She should not be with a group of horses, as some of them may pester and bother her when she starts to foal. She will want to get away by herself to have her foal in privacy.

One sign of approaching labor is the relaxing of the muscles on each side of the mare's tail. As the mare prepares herself for actual labor she may become quite restless and nervous. She may walk restlessly, fuss with her feed, sweat profusely, or just stand and tremble. She may switch her tail, or show other signs of discomfort.

Mares often foal at night, so if you suspect that her foaling time is near, it is well to check on her periodically throughout the night. This may mean several nights of checking if she doesn't foal right on schedule or shows signs of foaling several days before she actually goes into labor. Check on her every few hours, but do not alarm her or make her nervous. It is best to stay out of her sight and not let her know you are there. She will be less nervous and upset about her foaling if there are no distractions. If all seems to be going well, stay out of sight.

The mare should be kept well groomed and clean. The cleaner the mare, the less chance of infection when the genital tract is exposed during foaling, and the fewer harmful bacteria will be picked up by the foal as he noses about the mare to begin nursing. Many breeders wrap the mare's tail in a clean tail bandage when they clean her up for foaling; this prevents a lot of filth from coming in contact with the open genital tract as she foals, and also keeps the mare's tail clean and free from blood and mucus.

The mare should have her feed cut down for about a week before you think she will foal, and she should be kept on low rations for several days after foaling. The birth of the foal can be accomplished much easier if the mare is as empty as possible at that time. Another reason for cutting down her feed at foaling time is to decrease the milk flow; too heavy or too rich a diet at foaling time will usually cause a mare to produce too much milk. The foal won't be able to take all of her milk at first. If the milk is too rich or if the foal is getting too much milk, he will get scours (diarrhea).

When the mare begins to show signs of actual labor, do not feed her at all. Let her have a little water if she wants it, but not too much. Remember, she should be as empty as possible. After she foals it is best not to feed her again until you have had a chance to observe the foal's bowel movements to see if he will be scouring or not.

There are three stages of labor. The first stage is the longest and will take anywhere from four to twenty-four hours. It will take longer for a mare with her first foal than for one that has had foals previously. In this first stage of labor there are contractions of the uterus as the foal is shifted and turned into the correct position for birth. Once in a great while the foal will not be turned to the correct position, and the mare will have to be helped.

The inexperienced horseman should make arrangements to have a veterinarian or an experienced breeder present. Usually everything goes along according to nature's plan and the mare will have her foal safely with no trouble at all. But if problems arise, the inexperienced person should not rely on his own efforts to help the mare, or he may endanger the life of the foal and the mare both. The time to contact the vet is when the mare is in the first stage of labor. Keep him posted on progress so that he can be there when she goes into the second, or active stage.

During the first stage of labor the mare is usually restless, short-tempered, and nervous. Her pelvic muscles relax more fully, her tail rises, and her sides look "caved in" just ahead of the hip bones; the foal is shifting position and heading into the birth canal. As contractions occur, the mare will show distress, switching her tail, nervously pacing about, and perhaps nosing at her flank or grunting. When you observe these first signs of labor, it is time to bandage her tail, supply her with fresh, clean bedding, and then leave her in privacy.

The second, or active stage of labor is when the foal is expelled from the uterus in a series of hard contractions. This stage does not take very long. During the first stage of early labor, the mare moved around quite a bit and was fairly comfortable between contractions, but after she enters the second stage of labor she is more constantly uncomfortable and will move around less. When her bag of water has broken, the second stage of labor is in progress. After the bag of water has broken, the foal should come within five to thirty minutes. Cows can safely be in the second stage of labor for several hours, but not a mare. If a mare takes longer than twenty minutes, she needs help and she needs it right away. A first foal will often take a little longer than other foals, but if nothing has happened within thirty minutes after the bag of water has broken, the mare is in trouble.

The normal position for a foal being born is head first with forefeet extended. The front feet should be first to appear, and then the nose, tucked between them. Any deviation from this (head turned back, one or both front feet turned back, hind feet first, etc.) is abnormal and professional help will be needed at once, the sooner the better. A foal in an abnormal position cannot be born and it and the mare may both die (a foal coming hind feet first will be born all right, but may suffocate if the birth is not accomplished immediately). A foal in an abnormal position must be pushed back and turned to the proper position before it can be born, and this can be accomplished much easier if detected early. To push the foal back to where it can be turned or straightened out properly will be pushing against the mare's labor contractions and is very hard to do if part of the foal is already well along in the birth canal. If the foal is being presented wrong, do not attempt to correct the situation yourself if you are inexperienced, but get skilled help immediately.

If the foal is being presented normally, you must still keep in mind the fact that the delivery must take place very soon. Once in active labor, the mare must foal soon or the blood supply to the foal will be interfered with and it will die. If the foal is unusually big, or for some other reason the mare is taking too long, grasp the foal's forelegs and help the mare in the delivery. Pull strongly with each contraction. It is best to pull as she pushes; if you pull too hard when she is *not* pushing, you might injure the membranes of the birth canal. A long and difficult birth will tire both the mare and the foal. The more quickly the mare accomplishes her act of labor, the more quickly will she return to normal, and the better start the foal will have.

Mares usually foal lying down, but some do so standing up. If your mare is foaling in a stall rather than in a pasture, make sure she is in the center of the stall—whether she is standing or lying—with her hindquarters well away from the wall.

When the foal is born he will still be wrapped in membrane, but he should quickly free himself by his own struggles. If he does not immediately free himself, you should break the sac and wipe the mucus from his nose and mouth so that he can start breathing. Make sure that he is breathing normally.

The umbilical cord usually breaks when the mare gets up. If it doesn't you can pull the foal away from her until the cord breaks. Never cut or tie the cord, and do not touch it with your hands unless they are clean and disinfected. The blood vessels of the cord have greater elasticity than the outer covering; if the cord is broken rather than cut, these blood vessels will draw back into the stump of the navel and help seal off the opening to infection. Sometimes there will be considerable drainage of blood when the cord is broken, but this is no cause for alarm.

The stump of the foal's navel should be disinfected with tincture of iodine. This is done by saturating a piece of cotton with iodine and holding it firmly over the stump for a couple of minutes, or can be done easily with the foal in a standing position by placing a small jar or glass of iodine up to the navel stamp and making sure the entire stump is thoroughly dipped. Be careful not to spill any iodine on the foal; it burns. Disinfecting the navel with iodine is an important practice; it helps close the navel stump to infection and reduces the chance of joint ill and other problems. Do not touch the navel with your hands and do not tie it. There will be a certain amount of natural drainage; tying would prevent this and cause trouble.

Move the foal to the front of the mare if she has not yet arisen, so that she can see him and nose him. If the weather is quite cold you can dry the foal with a rough towel, but otherwise the mare will manage nicely. Remove any wet or soiled bedding, then leave the mare and foal alone. The mare will do a better job of mothering the foal (especially if it is her first) if there are few distractions to make her nervous.

The third stage of labor is when the mare expels the afterbirth. This should occur soon after foaling. If it takes her longer than two hours, this is abnormal. If she has not cleaned within eight hours after foaling, you should consult a veterinarian. The mare is in grave danger if she has not shed the afterbirth within twenty-four hours.

The afterbirth should always be checked for completeness, for if any part of it is retained inside the mare it will cause serious trouble. When the membranes are spread out they will look like a pair of trousers that have the end of the legs closed. There should be only one tear in the membrane and it will be at the "waist" of the "trousers." If any part of the membrane is missing (still within the mare) it will usually be the tip of one of the closed trouser "legs."

The foal should be on its feet and nursing within an hour after it is born. Make sure that the foal gets his first feeding. Do not rush him or force him; nature usually takes care of her own. Just stay out of sight and be patient. Eventually he will find the right place to nurse. But once in a great while you may need to assist if the foal is exceptionally tired (from a hard birth) or weak, or if the mare kicks at him. Sometimes a mare will kick if her udder is swollen and sore, but usually only half-heartedly and won't hurt the foal. Rarely will a mare kick viciously at a foal, but if this does happen you will need to intervene. A mare with her

First meal! (Nikki and Nell)

first foal may take a while before the foal succeeds in nursing; this nursing business is new to her and her udder may be sore and she may move around quite a bit.

If the foal has not succeeded in nursing by the time he is two hours old, you should help him before he gets tired and discouraged. If the foal is reluctant to nurse, or fails to nurse within eight hours, you should seek the advice and help of a vet.

The mare's first milk (colostrum) acts as a laxative for the foal and cleans out his intestinal tract. The colostrum also stimulates gastric and intestinal secretions in the foal. These secretions are harmful to certain kinds of bacteria and are important in warding off intestinal disturbances in the newborn foal. Unlike the human baby who picks up much of his mother's immunity while he is still in the womb, the foal is born without any resistance to infection. Also unlike the human baby, the foal has only a limited time in which to absorb immunities through the mother's milk; after that the foal's intestinal membranes are too thick. This is why it is very important to get the foal nursing as soon as possible, for the foal has only twenty-four to thirty-six hours after his birth to absorb resistance to disease through the colostrum. After a few weeks the foal is able to produce his own antibodies.

The foal's first bowel movements will be dark, and sometimes very hard (this is the material that was in the foal's intestines before he was

First romp in the pasture. (Nell and her firstborn foal Amahl)

Hello, World! (Fahleen and Nell)

Relaxing in the sun. (Nell and Amahl)

born; the foal continually swallows some of the fluid in which he floats, but never evacuates his intestinal tract until after he is born, so a great number of hard pellets accumulate in the intestines and are sometimes packed so hard that the foal has a hard time getting rid of them), then as the colostrum begins to work the bowel movements will become soft and yellow, but they should not become runny. A foal may die because the owner neglects to make sure its "innards" are working properly. If the foal doesn't have a bowel movement in a few hours it is wise to call a vet or some other qualified person to give the foal an enema. Constipation is one of the most common causes of death in newborn foals.

If the foal's bowel movements become runny, he is probably getting too much milk. This problem will correct itself if the mare is not fed excessively, and the foal will adjust to the mare's milk within a few days. But if scouring persists, and especially if the bowel movements are watery or of unnatural color, consult a vet; the foal might have an infection. He will become weak from loss of fluid if scouring persists for any length of time.

Within twenty-four hours (if possible) after foaling, turn the mare and foal out in a clean pasture if they are doing well. Both need exercise. After a few days they can be put into a pasture with other brood mares or mares and foals. You can start to use the mare again moderately about ten or twelve days after foaling.

10

RAISING AND TRAINING THE FOAL

That new foal you have been waiting for has safely arrived. Now let's look at those next few months—caring for that foal until he is weaned, and the beginning of his training.

For the first week or two after foaling, oat hay or green grass is usually enough feed for the mare. This tends to reduce the amount of milk she produces, which is helpful until the foal is able to handle all her milk, and until the mare has passed her first heat period, called "foal heat," which usually occurs about the ninth day after foaling. After that, grain (and alfalfa hay if the mare is on hay or poor pasture) may be added gradually to the mare's ration. Thin mares, or mares that don't produce enough milk, should be fed grain earlier.

Most foals scour a little at the time of the mare's first heat period. This diarrhea lasts from one to three days and is caused by the laxative effect of the milk at this time. No treatment is required for this diarrhea except to keep the foal's hindquarters clean and well-greased with vaseline or mineral oil to prevent irritation and loss of hair.

When the foal is a couple of weeks old and the mare is back on a normal diet, she should be fed a well-balanced and adequate diet. Nursing a foal takes a lot out of a mare; a good broodmare produces as much or more milk than a dairy cow, and is working harder than a race horse. She should be fed accordingly. Make sure she also has plenty of fresh, clean water. She may drink up to 15 or 20 gallons of water a day in order to keep up her milk flow. The amount she drinks will depend somewhat on how warm the weather is—she will drink much more in hot weather than in cold weather.

The foal can be started on grain at two and one-half to three weeks of age. He will usually nibble some of his mother's grain if you let him in with her while you feed her. He will soon get used to the taste of it and

121

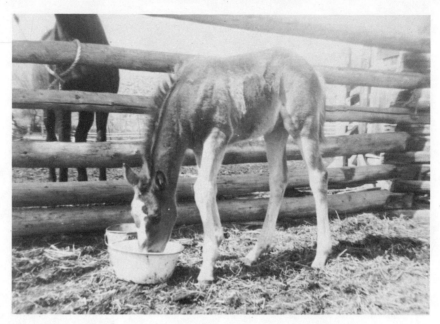

The foal can be started on grain at three weeks old.

begin eating it readily himself. When you start feeding him grain in earnest you will probably want to use a foal creep (an enclosure in the pasture with openings large enough for the foal to get in and eat the grain, but too small for the mare to get in) or a separate stall next to the mare's so the foal will be able to get his full ration and the mare won't eat most of his. A recommended feeding for the young foal is to start with half a pound of grain per day, gradually increasing it until at two or three months of age he is getting between one and two pounds per day. He should be getting nearly two and one-half pounds per day by weaning time. As with the feeding of any horse, it is best to divide the ration and feed it in two or even three feedings daily instead of all at once; it will do the foal much more good. Get a well-balanced grain mix that contains the necessary protein and vitamins and minerals for a growing foal. Many grains are high in carbohydrates but not in protein.

Foals grow quite fast. Unlike a calf that nurses two or three times during the day, the foal nurses every two or three hours. The average mare is producing a great deal of milk, and if she is separated from her foal for more than two or three hours her udder will become very full and uncomfortable. If you are using the mare again after she has her foal, you will want to work out a schedule that will not prove to be hard on the mare or her growing foal.

Worming should start at two months of age. Worms can rob the

Foals nurse every two or three hours and grow very rapidly.

growing foal of needed nutrition, making him thin, pot-bellied, or give him a shaggy, dull coat of hair. Bloodworms can do internal damage that won't show up until later. Treatment for several types of worms can begin at weaning time, but treatment for roundworms can start at two months of age. Consult your vet for an effective worming program.

If the mare has not been bred again, the foal can be weaned as late as eight or nine months. Some negligent horsemen leave a foal on the mare even longer than this. Most mares will wean the foal of their own accord before the foal becomes a yearling, but others don't, and to leave the foal on the mare any longer than this is not good for the mare.

If the mare is pregnant, the foal should be weaned at 5½ or six months of age. A pregnant mare still nursing a foal beyond six months will not do justice to both the foal she is carrying and the nursing foal. The extra strain will weaken her and make her anemic.

Weaning is best accomplished by completely separating the mare and foal so that they cannot see or hear one another. They will more quickly adjust to the situation if they are far apart than if they are constantly reminded of one another. If the foal has other weanlings for company, he will be happier. If he is by himself, another horse through the fence (not his mother) will help to keep him company. When you wean the foal, make sure the enclosures you select for him and for the mare are safe and hazard-free, with good smooth fencing. You don't want the foal to injure himself in his frantic efforts to get out and go to his mother. Some mares are just as frantic as their foals, so be sure the mare's enclosure is safe, too.

Some horsemen are too concerned with the comfort of the mare and her problem of "drying up" when the foal is weaned. They actually do not help her by milking her out, applying hot packs, rubbing the udder, etc. This merely stimulates her to make more milk. The udder will get full and swollen when the foal is taken away, but this pressure is necessary for the mare to dry up. Nature can then tell that the milk is no longer needed and the milk secretion will stop. If the udder becomes exceptionally swollen and painful, cold packs can be applied. Exercise and no grain for a week or more will help the mare dry up.

Weaning is not such a severe jolt to a foal if he has been fed a good portion of grain as a foal. He may go off feed a little for a day or so because of being upset, but he will soon bounce back. It is much easier for a foal to take weaning in stride if he has been fed regularly; he will be a bigger foal to begin with and will not have the added problem of learning to eat a strange feed at a time when he is upset over the loss of his mother. And the grain-fed foal will be happy to see you and the feed bucket!

It is easy to win the foal's confidence when he is very young. My little sister Heidi with Nell's fourth foal, Amahl II.

There are several schools of thought about when a horse's training should begin. Some people wait until the horse is a two-year-old or older before they do anything with him. Others begin handling the foal at birth, in the belief that the young horse will never forget his early training and that he will be easier to handle when he is older.

Being of the latter school, I like to see horses handled when they are young. The foal learns quickly and is easier to handle because he is not a great deal bigger and stronger than you are. A horse's fear and suspicion of man (and also his size and strength, don't forget!) increase with age; it is easier to win his confidence when he is young.

The first thing to gain the foal's confidence is to let him become accustomed to you. A box stall or very small corral is an ideal place to work with the foal and its mother. To begin with, work around the mare. Brush her or clean her feet while you talk quietly to the foal. As the little one gets used to your presence and is no longer afraid, handle him and get him accustomed to the feel of your hands. Don't force him; take your time. You don't need to fight and struggle with him; that will only make him more afraid of you. After a few days the foal will probably come to you of his own free will when you enter the mare's stall. If the mare is quiet and gentle and accepts you, the foal will soon do likewise.

A mare's instinct to protect her baby is strong, and she may lead him away from you when she is loose in the pasture. Don't be surprised or disappointed if your old trustworthy, "easy-to-catch" mare departs to far corners with her foal when you enter her pasture. Don't ever chase her or make her run with her baby. This only increases fear and may start bad habits for the foal. You may have to use grain to catch the mare until she gets into the habit of being readily caught again. You should be graining her daily anyway when she is nursing a foal; this will make her easy to catch, for she will be anticipating her grain.

You might have to tie the mare in the stall while you work with the foal, especially if she is nervous and worried about what you are doing to her baby.

An easy way to catch the foal is to corner him between you and the mare and the stall wall. The best way to hold him these first few times you catch him is with one arm around his chest or neck and the other arm around his buttocks. It is better to restrain him with your arms at first than to try to use a rope or a halter; you will be less likely to hurt him or get him tangled up if he struggles. Foals can move very fast when they are frightened, and they are not as apt to watch where they are going as an older horse. You don't want the foal running into the stall wall and injuring himself because you have too much slack in the rope when he jumps, and so forth. Until he is more accustomed to you, don't

Using a loop "come-along" behind the foal's hindquarters to teach him to lead.

try ropes or halters. It is better to restrain the foal by holding him around the body than by taking a chance on hurting his head or neck in his struggles to pull away from you.

It is customary to work from the left side when handling horses, but it is also a good idea to have the foal accustomed to being handled from either side. After he is used to you and accepts you without fear, you will be able to put a halter on him. Let him wear it for a short while the first time in order to get used to it—preferably in the box stall. Don't turn him loose in the pasture with a halter on. Always be sure that the halter you use on a foal is close-fitting; never use one that is loose-fitting or too large for him, or he may snag it on something or get a hind foot through it when scratching his ear, or a front foot through it by pawing at it.

A foal grows so fast that it's hard to keep his halter the proper size. I've found it handy to use several sizes. One is a halter that is quite small and is adjustable for the smallest foal's head and which can be let out and worn until about five or six months of age. I have another that the foal can wear until he is a yearling. After that a small pony or yearling halter works until he outgrows it and graduates to a regular size halter at age two or three, depending on the size of the horse.

After you have gained the foal's confidence, he won't mind letting you halter and unhalter him or move your hands over his body and up and down his legs. Always move slowly and deliberately; sudden movements will startle him.

Most young horses learn to lead easily, and since at this stage you are probably as strong as he is, the task is not too difficult. The proper way to lead a horse is to walk beside his left shoulder. The foal will lead almost naturally, walking beside you, until you try to lead him away from his mother and out of sight of her. You can avoid his struggling and fighting by using a loop of rope or a leather strap around his buttocks. When he balks, pull on the loop. He soon learns that the easiest thing to do is to move forward when the loop begins to tighten around his hindquarters. Keep the loop slack when he moves out freely; use pressure only when he balks. But be sure it is not so slack that it hangs down and annoys his hocks as he walks.

After several lessons he will move out well when you lead him and you can soon tell when to dispense with the "come-along" loop around his hindquarters. Occasionally a foal will regress if he is frightened by something or if you come to a strange object he does not want to walk past. In this case you may have to resort to using the loop "come-along" again for a short time.

Whenever you tie the foal, be sure it is with something strong and

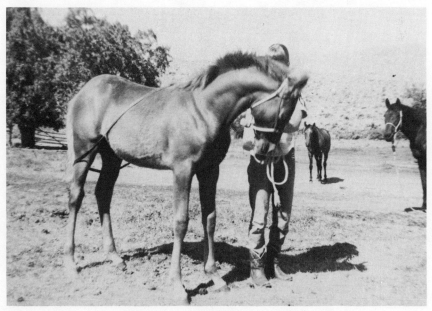

The foal in these pictures is Fahleen.

solid that will hold him. This is always wise, even when tying an older, well-halter-broken horse. A horse can have a terrible scare if he ever sets back on something that comes loose and drags along with him. An experience like this may make him a habitual halter-puller. Even a well-trained horse may set back if something spooks him, so it's always a good idea to tie solid.

The first few times you tie the foal, use a body rope instead of just tying him by the halter. Don't tie him by the neck. If you use a body rope the foal will not be so likely to hurt his neck muscles when he sets back

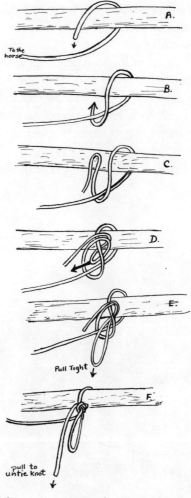

A. The end of the halter rope goes under the pole. B. The rope goes under itself. C. Double the end of the rope into a loop. D. Stick the loop through the first loop. E. Pull the loop through and pull it tight. F. The finished knot. To untie it, pull the end of the rope.

or struggles. A body rope consists of a loop of rope that goes around his girth, with the free end coming out between his front legs. I like to tie a solid knot rather than a slip knot in the loop that goes around his middle, so that the loop will not tighten and squeeze him when he pulls back. If he pulls back steadily or falls down, a slip knot will keep tightening, making it hard for him to breathe, and also making it very difficult for you to undo the knot to free the foal. The free end of the rope goes between the foal's front legs and through the halter ring to tie him with. Thus, when he pulls back and tries to get free, most of the strain will come on his body and not only on his head and neck.

When you tie the foal be sure that the rope is not too long, or he may have enough slack to get a foot over the rope or to go over backward and fall down in his struggles. Tie him high and short. Always tie to something level with his head or higher. If the rope is tied low he may injure his neck when he pulls. There is also more danger of his getting a front foot over the rope if it is low, especially if he paws at it. Make sure there are no sharp or harmful objects that he might run into as he fights the rope.

A good knot to use when tying a horse is the manger tie. See the accompanying illustration if you don't know how to tie it. This is a good

Tied up with a "body rope." Three-weeks-old Fahleen . . . very impatient about the whole thing.

knot to use because it can always be pulled free in a hurry in an emergency. If the foal falls down in an awkward or dangerous position during his struggles, you can untie him to free him instead of cutting the rope; the manger tie can still be untied even when there is much pressure on the rope that would make other knots difficult to loosen. When tying a foal, or any horse that nibbles or plays with the rope, run the loose end of the rope through the loop in the manger-tie knot. This will keep the knot from coming undone if the foal loosens it by playing with the rope.

Stay nearby the first few times you tie the foal, so that you can get him out of a bind if necessary. If he falls down in his struggles he may not be able to get up by himself, especially if the rope is holding him at an awkward angle. Always tie with a knot that can be undone in a hurry no matter how tight it gets.

But the rope should be the final master. The foal must not be rewarded with his freedom during his struggles or he will think that he can always free himself by fighting and struggling. If you do have to untie him to get him out of a bad position, tie him up again. Soon after he ceases fighting and submits to the fact that he must stand there, turn him loose. Don't leave a young foal tied up for any great lengths of time, especially during the first lessons. One or two lessons a day for a couple of weeks will make him respect the halter and rope. Most foals will be completely halter broken (and stay that way) after this first series of lessons.

When you first pick up the foal's foot, he won't know how to balance on three legs and you will have to lean on him a little to get him to shift his weight. If he feels himself off balance he will probably try to take his foot away, but do not let him—taking his foot away from you can become a very bad habit. Lean into him to help steady his balance. After several times he will learn to shift his weight himself when you start to pick up a foot. Picking up a front foot upsets his balance even more than picking up a hind, for the horse carries more of his weight on his front feet.

In everything you do with the foal, frequent short lessons are more valuable than occasional long ones. Handle the foal regularly. After he learns what you want him to do, his reactions will become more and more automatic. By the same token, if you confuse or frighten him and he reacts adversely to what you are trying to do (or if you let him get away with bad manners repeatedly) it is easy for the reaction to become a bad habit. Try to make the foal understand what you want him to do. Most horses are willing to learn, up to a point. After that they become tired and give up.

Never work with the foal after he has become tired and has ceased to give you his attention, or he will begin to dislike the whole routine

Two-months-old Nikki . . . learning to stand quietly while tied.

and you'll discover that you've undone a lot of the training. Perhaps one of the most important aspects of being a good horse trainer is knowing when to quit. You have to be able to sense your pupil's mood and end the lesson on a good note while he is still trying and learning and doing things right, rather than waiting too long and having to quit after he is tired and starting to fight you or is doing things wrong. This is an important point in training horses of any age.

And remember that each horse is an individual. No two will act alike. What worked well in training one foal might not do for another. You will have to use good judgment and sometimes a lot of ingenuity as well. There will be a difference in character, even in horses that are closely related; you can't expect them to all react alike. Some are affectionate, others are very independent. Some foals are quite sassy.

And while we're on this subject, we'd better mention the problems of spoiling. A spoiled foal is often worse to handle than a timid or frightened foal. The timid foal can be controlled and taught that nothing will hurt him so long as he behaves. But the spoiled foal is not afraid of anything. He knows that no one is going to hurt him, no matter what he does; this foal can grow up to be a very bad-mannered or even dangerously mean horse.

Most foals are inquisitive, playful and sassy. Unless corrected, these traits can become very bad habits. The small foal who nips playfully

Teaching the foal to pick up its feet.

at your clothes may seem cute, but he won't be so cute when he is larger than you are and takes a hunk out of your skin. Nor will he be so cute if he "playfully" kicks at you when he is an 800-pound two-year-old. If you use tact and good judgment you can often keep from giving that foal the opportunity to bite or kick at you. This is important because there are many times when you won't be in a position to punish or correct him; it is very bad to let him kick or nip and then run off. You are not able to punish him effectively until you have him under control (haltered or tied or in a very small pen or stall), for you don't want him to get the idea he can get away from you. When he does nip or kick, a sharp slap on the muzzle or on the rump can be quite effective. Just be sure the punishment immediately follows the misdeed. But don't overdo it. Never strike the foal above the muzzle or around the ears, or you may make him head-shy. Foals can be devilishly quick; they can often get in a nip and away again before you can punish. So you must be quick. Better yet is to be able to anticipate a nip and prevent it. You must be able to outsmart the foal.

Many foals will go through exasperating stages of being nippy or hard to catch, or in other ways uncooperative. But do not become discouraged. With tact and good judgment, the foal will soon outgrow these little bad habits. Patience is so important, and so is *time*. A good horseman has both. Have a goal in mind and always work toward it, but don't feel disappointed if you see no progress at some points. Time is on your side.

The high-strung, sensitive foal needs more handling and a little more time and patience than the less sensitive one. In many ways it is more frustrating to train a sensitive, highly intelligent horse that has a great deal of pride; it may take longer to gain his confidence, but once you do you are truly a team. In spite of the frustrations, there is a lot more joy in training one of these animals than in training a duller, more easygoing one, for the proud and sensitive horse has more potential, and when *well* trained he will continually be a source of amazement and inspiration to you. An independent and proud horse will give you some exasperating moments as you try to train him; he can never be "broken" for he is too proud and will only become resentful and fight you if you try to force him. But with good intelligent training and patience, he can be "bent" to your will, and once he does gain confidence in you there is practically no limit to what he can do. Often these very independent horses have more "heart" than others, and turn in amazing performances wherever they are used—on the track, on the jump course, on endurance rides, in the show ring, or just putting in a long strenuous day working cattle in the mountains.

If we are going to work with horses we should try to understand them—to understand why a horse reacts as he does to the way we handle him. A good horseman is sensitive to his horse's behavior. He knows how much his horse can do and will not make demands beyond its ability. He knows when to punish and when to be patient.

Repetition, memory, and habit are the main factors we deal with in training a horse. When training a horse, the first thing we must do is get his attention, then we try to make him understand what we want him to do. Training is based partly upon reward and punishment, and upon repetition of what we want the horse to do. The foal learns to do a certain thing a certain way by repetition. It becomes habit. But if he does it wrong, we must punish him so that he will not make the same mistake. Bad behavior can become habit, too, if we let him get away with it often enough. He should be rewarded for good behavior and punished *only* when he misbehaves. The reward—a pat and a friendly voice, or a slacking up on the rope so that the foal can relax—should immediately follow the act of obedience. For example, after the foal has stood quietly for a while after being tied, he should be patted and turned loose. Or, if he has walked out freely for several steps when you are teaching him to lead, he should be rewarded by slack on the rump rope "come-along" and by kind words, etc. The punishment, to be effective, must immediately follow the misdeed. If he misbehaves, such as fighting the rope when tied, he should be left tied until he ceases fighting. If he bites, kicks, paws at the rope, or in some other way misbehaves, he should be punished each time until he learns not to do it.

The horse's memory is not very long, and if you punish him after a few minutes have gone by, he may not know the reason. This is why it is important always to have the horse under control; if he can get away from you or dodge the punishment, it will do no good to punish him after you catch up with him; he will not know why you are punishing and it will only make him more afraid of you.

Punishment is not justifiable if the foal is irritated because his halter does not fit properly or if some other rope or equipment is hurting him. Nor is punishment justified if he reacts to you out of fear or shies at something that frightens him.

A good trainer never punishes through anger. The foal may frustrate you at times, but if you can't control your temper, you will never be a horse trainer. All too often the punishment that is given in anger is for something the horse does through ignorance or fear, and he will not understand why he is being punished and only become more fearful.

Never ask a horse to do something that he cannot do—something beyond his ability or training—and if at any time you realize that you have, certainly do not punish him for his failure to perform. This will only confuse him. And never work with him after he has become tired or he will no longer give you his full attention. You should choose a quiet place in which to work with the foal, a place where his attention will not be distracted by strange, noisy surroundings or by other horses.

Now let's look at several other things you may want to teach the foal while he is small.

Teaching the foal to lead at the trot isn't hard. As you are leading him, give him the signal to trot by moving your feet faster (trotting in place, so to speak) and then begin to move faster yourself. After a few times the foal will catch on and begin to trot as soon as you give the signal. If he balks, you may need to carry a little switch in your other hand with which to tap his rump when you start to trot. This is often necessary when teaching older horses to lead at the trot, and works quite well. Usually the foal catches on much more rapidly than an older horse; most foals I have trained did not require the switch at all.

It is better to use the switch than the loop around his buttocks, for the loop may bother his legs as he trots, especially if you get too much slack in it. You don't want him distracted by a loop flapping his hocks or constantly urging him forward and faster by rubbing or bumping his buttocks. Most foals are quite lively, and often the main problem is not so much getting them to trot as it is to hold them down to a trot after they start off. Never let the foal get up too much speed, or he may get away from you; he can gallop a lot faster than you can!

After several lessons you will be able to move him right out into a trot from a standstill by giving the signal to trot with your feet. It's good to teach the foal to lead at both the walk and the trot; it makes him more agile and maneuverable and responsive to restraint. It is especially good if you ever plan to show him at halter. It's no fun to have to drag him along at the end of his lead shank when it's your turn to trot him for the judge (among other things, it will show his lack of training), and the judge won't be able to get a good view of his action if you are out in front of the horse.

To teach the foal to back up, pull back gently on his halter. It will help if you turn so that you are facing him and can push on his chest or shoulder with one hand as you pull backward on his halter with the other. At the same time, give the command "Back." Always use the same tone of voice when you give the command. He will begin to associate the command with backing and after a few lessons should back up readily when the command is given and there is a backward pull on his halter. But don't rush him. Even one step backward should be rewarded so that he knows he is doing the right thing. Just ask for one step at a time and stop the lesson after he has successfully made three or four steps backward.

The first several times you groom the foal will be mostly for training, for you won't get a great deal of real grooming done. When starting out, just rub him with your hand. He will probably enjoy it. When he is accustomed to your hand, try a soft cloth. Show it to him first, and after he sees that it isn't going to hurt him, rub various parts of his body with it. Then try a brush. It is easiest to start at the withers and along the back, then up the neck. Most horses are touchy about their faces, so take it easy there. Work around the croup and under the stomach and gradually down the legs. When you come to a touchy spot, slow down and work to that place again. You probably can't do it all in one day. You are doing a lot of training that must be done before you can really do a good job of grooming.

If the foal is halter-broken, you can tie him to keep him in one place while you groom him. As he learns to like it, he will stand without being tied. But a word of caution: the foal can develop some bad habits which may seem cute at first, but later on they aren't so cute. If he is tied, don't let him chew on the rope. Don't let him chew on the brush or nibble at you. If he is not tied, don't let him walk around. He should learn to stand quietly. Bring him back to the same spot and insist that he stand there. A slap on the chest and the word "Whoa" whenever he starts to move forward will usually cure him of wandering.

The foal seems to like to hear his name and becomes attentive when he hears it. He learns his name by hearing it repeated often in such a way that he knows you are speaking to him.

Your voice is important in training a horse; it isn't what you say that matters, but the tone of voice. It should be soft and soothing; the word "Easy" is a good one for the foal to learn—it will often save you trouble later on when you get into situations where you need to calm and reassure him. A strong, severe voice should be used only for reprimands.

Some foals learn very rapidly, others more slowly. You will have to work out your individual training program for each as you go along. Your foal may be a very fast learner, but don't make the mistake of trying to teach him too much at one time. Don't confuse him. Be sure that he has learned one thing well before you go on to something new. Remember to keep your actions slow so that he won't be startled. He doesn't understand what you are doing at first and everything is strange to him, so take it slow.

A foal will never forget his early training, even if you don't have time to do much more with him after those first lessons until he is a year or two older. But when he is older he will be a great deal easier to handle and to continue training because he will have trust and confidence in you. He will turn to you in difficult situations and trust you to get him out of them instead of blindly fighting and plunging. Early training is a good foundation for the later work you will do with a horse, whether you are training him as a pleasure horse, stock horse, show horse, trail horse, hunter or jumper. He will be easier to train because he will accept new things readily and his reaction to what you do with him will be out of confidence rather than fear.

11

BEFORE YOU RIDE

As mentioned in the previous chapter, there are many ways to train a horse and several schools of thought about how it should be done. But there are two basic facts to keep in mind. First, any early training that you give a horse when he's a foal or a yearling makes you just that much farther ahead when the day comes to start riding him. The young horse never forgets his early training; he'll be more ready to trust you, more used to being handled, and it will be helpful to have him gentle, halter-broken, and willing to lead and to do your bidding when the time comes to work with him in earnest.

Second, don't ride him too soon. Many horsemen make the mistake of starting a young horse under saddle too young, before he is physically up to it. Some horses get their growth faster than others; a Quarter Horse generally matures faster than an Arabian, for instance. But as a general rule, a horse should not be put into extensive or rigorous training or ridden hard until he is four years old or older. Bones and tendons are still in the formative stage up to three years of age, the bones in the knee are not fully calcified until the horse is three, and if you'll recall from the chapter on splints, the splint bones are not firmly attached until the horse is five or six. These growing bones and tendons can be injured by heavy use, fast turns, and the like. This is why so many young horses get splints, bowed tendons, curbs, and other ailments that can become unsoundnesses.

I like to start my own horses under saddle as long two-year-olds or early three-year-olds, riding them a little mainly just to get them used to having someone on their back, and to get them moving out freely at the walk and trot, and perhaps a little at the canter. I start reining them a little (with snaffle bit or hackamore) and use leg pressure to help in guiding them around wide turns.

137

As long three-year-olds they get more extensive training—neck reining, backing, stopping, maintaining even speed at gaits, etc.—but still taking it easy on the fast work. There is a great deal a person can teach a horse before he needs to pour on the coal, and the horse will be more ready for fast work when he is mature.

I don't use a horse extensively until he is four or even older, working stock in rough country, making long and strenuous rides checking range cattle, polishing up his reining and maneuverability. To work him hard in his early years will only shorten his usefulness later, and I don't think it's worth it. We might see many more sound and useful horses in their late teens and twenties if horsemen didn't start them too young.

There is much that can be taught the horse even before he ever wears a saddle. As a yearling or two-year-old he can be taught to longe, to rotate on the forehand and on the quarters, and to drive in long lines. This groundwork is not absolutely necessary before you ride the horse, but the more work you do with the horse before you ride will make him just that much farther along when you actually do start riding him. Whether or not you do much groundwork depends on your own preferences and on your time. Several of my young horses have been started with thorough groundwork, some of my others have not (I do use a bitting harness and also drive each horse in long lines, however, whether or not I have time for other preparatory work such as longeing or teaching to rotate on forehand and quarters). It really makes no significant difference in the long run; it just gives the young horse a head start and will make some phases of mounted training much easier.

The word "longe" (pronounced "lawnj" or "lunj") means to exercise a horse with a long line. It can be one phase in the young horse's training, and can also be a good way to exercise any horse, young or old, that you don't have time to ride.

Longeing can be useful in starting a young horse, for it teaches him voice commands—walk, trot, canter and whoa—which can be helpful to you later when you start him under saddle. After he is used to being saddled, you can longe him with the saddle on to get him used to carrying it at various gaits. And before you mount him the first time, you can longe him for a while to get him warmed up and a little tired and he won't be so apt to buck.

For longeing a horse you will need a longeing caveson (but an ordinary halter will do if you don't have one), a long rope or longe line about twenty-five feet long with a swivel clip on the end that fastens to the halter, and a longeing whip or long willow switch. You will also need a small enclosure—preferably a round corral of some sort. For the first few lessons a round enclosure will let the horse get the idea of traveling in a circle, and will also keep him "light" on the line instead of pulling on it to try to make a larger circle. A square enclosure can be used, but is not as good as a round one, for the horse can get into a corner. After the horse has learned to longe, you can longe him anywhere, even in a pasture, but until he gets the idea, you will need a small enclosure.

The first step in teaching a horse to longe is to make him circle around you, and this can be accomplished easiest if you use a short rope at first. Hold the lead rope in one hand and the whip in the other (the rope in your left hand if he is going to the left and in your right hand if he is going to the right), and stand alongside the horse's flank. You want to be slightly to the rear so you can keep him going and keep him from turning to face you. And he will turn to face you or want to come to you until he understands that he is supposed to travel in a circle around you.

To make the horse move, say "Walk," raise the line in your hand so it will more or less "lead" him, and tap him gently on the hind-quarters with the whip. After he circles readily in that direction, you can stop him by saying "Whoa" and giving a quick pull on the line. For the first few lessons these two things, walking and stopping, are

Khamette as a two-year-old learning to work on a longe line.

enough to work on until he responds readily and well. Longe him to the right as often as you do to the left so that he will learn to go in both directions.

When the horse is making small circles around you (while he is still on the short rope or lead rope), don't let him go any faster than a walk or a very slow trot. A fast trot or a canter in a small circle is not good because he may injure his legs; he may strain them or may cause a splint by striking one leg with his other foot. Don't work too long during these first lessons; ten to twenty minutes is sufficient, and the horse will not become tired or bored.

After the horse circles both ways readily on the short rope, change to the longe line so you can gradually let him make bigger circles. Keep him out in the circle; point the whip at his quarters to keep him moving if he slows or to encourage him to stay out in the circle if he wants to face you or come to you.

When you want him to trot, say "Trot" and tap him on the hindquarters with the switch to encourage him to move faster. When he knows what the whip means, you will merely have to point it at him to get the desired response. This is important, because when he is out in the large circle you will not be able to reach him with the whip. And you will want to have him in a very large circle for trotting and cantering, to avoid injury to his legs. You can teach him to canter by giving the verbal command and pointing the whip to encourage him to move even faster. At first it will be easiest to make him break into a canter from a trot, but after he learns the command, you can make him canter from a walk or even from a standstill.

While you are teaching him to longe you may find at one point that he is reluctant to go in one direction or the other and he will stop and face you. But if you stay slightly to the rear and tap him from behind with the switch when he tries to face you, you can keep him moving. Another helpful suggestion: don't always stop him in the same place or always give a certain command as he reaches a certain part of the circle, or he may think that that place is the only spot he can do that particular thing. Avoid this from the very beginning and you'll save a lot of trouble; the horse should learn that he must obey the commands wherever and whenever they are given.

You can also teach him the command "Come here." After you have given the command "Whoa" and he has stood for a moment or so (and you will always want to let him stand a moment at "Whoa" before going on to a new command, so he'll get the idea that "Whoa" means *stop* and stay stopped) tell him to "Come here" and pull and slack on the line until he gets the idea and comes to you. At all other times he should be made to stay clear out in the circle.

In teaching voice commands, always use a firm, clear voice, and be consistent in how you intone each command; the horse understands the tone of your voice more than the words. You will only confuse him if you give the same command in several different ways.

More groundwork you can teach the young horse is rotation on his forehand and on his quarters. This will be of help later when you are trying to teach him to be more maneuverable, as when opening gates, teaching him elementary dressage movements, or turning on his haunches to make a speedier turn when cutting cattle, etc., and to respond to leg pressure by moving the appropriate part of his body in the desired direction.

To teach him to turn on his forehand, stand facing him at his left shoulder, with the lead rope held in the left hand about ten inches from his halter. Using your right hand, put pressure on the horse's side at about the same place the calf of your leg would be if you were mounted. Try to get the horse to move only his hindquarters away from you. You'll probably have to pull his head toward you a little to accomplish this. At the first "give" of his hindquarters, let him relax and let him know he has pleased you. Repeat this several times, getting him to make several side steps with his hindquarters. Do the same thing on the other side of him so he will learn to rotate either way. Don't work with him too long at one time.

To rotate him on the quarters, you'll need two lead ropes attached to his halter like reins. Put them over his neck. Face the same direction as the horse standing at his left shoulder, and take the right rope in your right hand and the left one in your left. Use them both to the side and a little to the rear to make him move only his front quarters to the left. He probably won't understand at first and you must have patience and keep trying until he does. When he does make that first step toward you with one of his front feet, give him a pat and a kind word and let him know he has done the right thing. Repeat the process, getting him to make two or more steps, then do the same thing on the other side.

You should rotate the horse on his forehand and on his quarters during the same lesson each time. If you do just one or the other or concentrate on one more than the other when you are teaching him, he may not learn to do both but rather think that he can only rotate one end.

It's all right if there is some up and down movement of the feet in the stationary end of him during either rotation, as long as there is no side movement.

It is good to get the young horse accustomed to the saddle (and to the bridle if you are starting him in a bit) before you ride him. When you saddle the horse for the first time, move slowly but confidently.

Don't scare him unnecessarily, yet go about it as though this were an everyday thing. Get him used to having the saddle blanket or pad put on and off several times before you try the saddle. After he stands quietly for putting on the saddle pad, gently set the saddle on his back. These first times you saddle him be especially careful to keep the stirrup and cinch from flopping down and hitting him on the off side. A well-trained and well-mannered horse stands quietly for saddling, but if you startle him several times with a flopping saddle he will be jumpy.

When the cinch is being tightened, the young horse may become afraid or upset, so be careful and move slowly. Check him and talk to him reassuringly if he begins to resent the saddle. Have the cinch tight enough to hold the saddle in place; you don't want him to have the frightening experience of losing it or having it slip if he should try to jump or buck with it.

But don't make the mistake of having it too tight. A tight cinch is very irritating to a horse, especially a young horse that isn't used to the saddle. The young horse overcomes his fear of strange new things if he is not hurt by them in any way.

Walk him around with the saddle on, then lead him at both the walk and the trot. Some trainers turn the young horse loose with the saddle on in a corral for awhile so that the horse can get used to stirrups flapping and to teach the horse that he can't get rid of the saddle even if he runs and bucks. This is not necessary, however. I feel it is better to never let the horse realize he *can* buck with the saddle or you on his back. If you build the foundation of his training properly and never give him the opportunity to buck, you'll never have to fight him when you're in the saddle and he will never find out that he can buck with you.

You will start your young horse in a hackamore or bit, depending on your preference. A well-halter-broken horse will usually start right out in a hackamore without much trouble. After you have taught him the principles of working in a hackamore, a bit can be hung in a light headstall under the hackamore (a snaffle bit is best) and you can gradually work him into the bit using four reins—gradually using the bit reins more than the hackamore reins.

"Bitting" is a good idea if you are going to start your horse in a bit, and is a valuable procedure even if you have already started the horse in a hackamore. Bitting teaches the horse to "give" to the bit instead of fighting it or lugging on it. Never use a severe bit on a young horse; it bruises the bars of the mouth and deadens the nerves, making a hard-mouthed horse if you have to use it forcefully, and there *will* be times you will need to use the bit harder with a green horse

Khamette as a two-year-old with saddle on for the first time.

Nikki in bitting harness as a two-year-old.

than you would with a trained horse for the green horse does not yet completely understand all that he is supposed to do. Therefore it is best to use the mildest bit possible.

The best way to get a horse accustomed to the bit is to use a bitting harness, for it does not hurt the horse's mouth, yet teaches him to "give" to the bit. A satisfactory bitting harness can be improvised or made from materials that you probably have on hand, and therefore won't cost much.

A bitting harness consists of a headstall and snaffle bit (broken snaffle is best), surcingle or bellyband, an overcheck to keep the horse from getting his head down, and side checks made from an elastic material such as strips of old rubber inner tubing that stretch when the horse tries to pull and root away from the bit. The elastic side checks won't hurt the tender mouth when the horse tries to pull on the bit (they are a lot better than ordinary side checks that do not stretch; with ordinary side checks the horse runs into a "solid" bit when he moves his head and can bump his mouth badly). The elastic side checks allow the horse to pull on the bit, yet they bring the horse's head right back into place. Soon he learns to relax his jaw and neck and "give" to the bit. A saddle can be used in place of a surcingle, using the horn to attach the overcheck, and attaching the side checks to the cinch rings.

This is the beginning of "collection"—a horse flexing at the poll

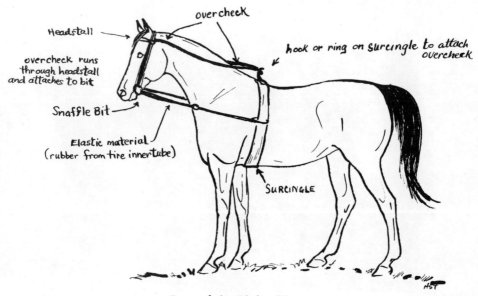

Parts of the Bitting Harness

Khamette (as a long two-year-old) in the bitting harness, "trying it out" and learning to "give" to the bit. It pulls her back each time she roots her nose forward.

and giving to the bit. Collection involves a great deal, including alertness and animation, and we will cover it more fully in a later chapter. A horse that is collected is "up on the bit" and "on his toes," so to speak; he is more able to be right where you want him at the right time.

When starting a young horse in a bit, make sure his headstall fits him properly. If you have a halter on him too, for leading him or longeing him with the bitting harness on, use a close-fitting halter under the headstall. The cheek straps of the headstall should be just tight enough that the snaffle bit wrinkles the corners of the mouth a little. You don't want it too tight, but you must have it tight enough that the horse cannot get his tongue over the bit. Be gentle and careful, but firm, when you put the headstall and bit on the young horse the first few times. You want him to learn to take the bit readily, so you won't want to make him headshy by rough handling of his ears, etc.

When you put the horse in the bitting harness, let him wear it around in a corral for a while so he can fully try it out and discover that it is easier to relax his jaw and give to the bit than to fight it. After he is used to the bitting harness (after several sessions of wearing it) you can lead or longe him in it. Thirty minutes or an hour each day

Khamette (after graduating from the bitting harness) has learned to relax her neck and jaw and does not fight the bit. Note the good flexion at the poll. Her mouth is soft and responsive to the bit.

in the bitting harness for several days will make a lot of difference and save a lot of work (and his mouth!) when you start riding him.

I like to drive a horse in long lines before I ride him. This is the next step after the bitting harness and teaches the horse to move out, stop, and turn. No matter what the horse is used for later, he will learn it faster if he has been taught these basic lessons at the start. The more a horse knows *before* you get on his back, the less confused he will be and the quicker he will learn what you want him to do.

To drive a horse in long lines, you can use either a hackamore or a snaffle bit. Hackamore does *not* mean a hackamore "bit," and snaffle does *not* mean a curb bit with jointed mouth, nor any bit with shanks. If you have not started the horse with a bitting harness, you might want to drive him in a hackamore. But if you have laid the foundation with sessions in a bitting harness and he has learned to flex and give to the bit, he will do fine driving in a bit.

A large corral is a good place to drive him. Don't drive him out in the open the first few times; in case of spooking or accident, you don't want him to have room to run or get away. Put driving lines on him, running them through the guides in the surcingle or through the stirrup bows if you have a saddle on him. This will keep them in place so there will be no danger of his getting a foot over them or otherwise

Driving in long lines.

getting fouled up. If you are using a saddle, tie the stirrups (you can either tie them down to the cinch rings or tie them together under the horse's belly).

At first you will need someone to lead the horse while you drive him, for he isn't used to someone behind him and may want to turn around and come to you instead of moving out. After he gets the idea he will move out freely without anyone leading him.

Start him with a slap of the reins or a touch of the whip (your voice commands from longeing can come in handy!) and let him go at random for a few minutes so he can get accustomed to someone following him. To stop him, use a slight seesaw pull on the reins and give the command "Whoa." Give the lines slack when he stops, and let him stand a while each time you stop him, so that he knows that the signal to stop means to stop completely.

When you want to start him, take up the slack in the lines and speak to him. Give him the command to walk, and slap him gently with the lines if he doesn't move. Drive him in a circle both ways, and start him with you standing to one side or the other, to get him used to seeing you on both sides. Until he learns to turn well (turn him by a pull on the rein in the direction you want him to go, pulling his head around) you can use the corral fence as an aid, turning him one way or the other when he gets to the fence. After he drives well in the corral you

The lines go through the stirrup bows.

can drive him at the trot as well as the walk, and can also drive him out in the open or in a pasture.

Up to this point you have been preparing him for the day you will get on and ride. Now he should be ready. He is used to the saddle and bridle, and knows the fundamentals of turning, moving, and stopping on your command. If you have carefully laid the groundwork for riding, the next step will be accomplished with ease.

12

STARTING THE YOUNG HORSE UNDER SADDLE

You have worked with your horse in preparation for starting him under saddle. He is well halter-broken, and has been bitted in a bitting harness and driven in long lines so that he knows that a pull on the left rein means a turn to the left, a pull on the right rein means a turn to the right, and a pull on both reins means stop.

Now the big day has arrived when you will ride him for the first time. These first few rides are quite important in setting the stage for the rest of his training, so you should take special care to make them go well. Saddle and bridle him as before, taking care that all equipment fits properly and does not pinch the horse in any way. For the first few rides, I like to put a close-fitting halter under the bridle and tie the halter rope to the saddle horn, with slack enough that it doesn't interfere with his normal movements of head and neck, but tight enough that he can't get his head down far enough to really buck. Walk him around a little to get him used to the feel of the saddle and bridle.

For the first rides, a corral or other small enclosure is best; the horse doesn't have room to do much running and won't be able to get clear away from you if something happens.

The first mounting is important. You'll want to accomplish it without startling or frightening the horse. It is best if you can manage it yourself without having someone hold the horse for you; being held for mounting can lead to the bad habit of not standing still for mounting in the future. If you have thoroughly taught the horse what "Whoa" means (during driving and longeing lessons) and have made him stand still for you during grooming and other work you have done with him, you probably won't have any trouble.

Talk to the horse, handle him, get him relaxed and standing still for you as you putter around him, straightening stirrups, pulling stirrup leathers, putting weight in the saddle, working on either side, and so forth. When the horse is calm and ready, go ahead and mount. Do it smoothly and easily, taking care to keep your leg from dragging across his rump or letting your weight down into the saddle suddenly, for this would startle him. Keep a short rein so you can check him if he starts to move. Some trainers like to check the horse's head around as they mount the first times, turning his head back toward them with left hand on the headstall and right hand on the saddle horn for mounting. This keeps the horse from moving forward while the rider mounts, but usually won't be necessary if you have done some work with him already so that he is well-mannered and knows the meaning of "Whoa." If the horse begins to get excited or frightened as you start to mount, back down again and calm him. When he is reassured and no longer nervous, try it again.

After you are in the saddle, if the horse does not move, just sit there a moment and talk quietly to him, rub him, get him used to your being up there. Then dismount and mount again, repeating this several times so that he learns it is nothing to fear.

If he moves out while you are in the saddle, let him. You can get him accustomed to lots of mounting and dismounting later. For the moment, just let him move at will for a while, getting used to the extra weight of a person on his back.

Many horses do not move out of their own accord when mounted the first time; they are rather bewildered and stand as though rooted to the ground. After you have practiced mounting and dismounting several times and are ready to move him out, squeeze him a little with your legs. Don't kick or use your heels, and don't put pressure back toward his flanks. Just squeeze with the calves of your legs as they hang naturally in the stirrups slightly to the rear of the cinch. If he still doesn't move, turn his head a little, pulling it to the side and down a little with one rein. This will usually put him off balance a little and he will have to take a step.

The first step he takes with an unaccustomed weight on his back may thoroughly frighten him, for your weight makes his balance entirely different. Speak reassuringly to him. Allow him to take several steps (and be prepared to halt him at any time he becomes frightened enough to spook or buck). After he has walked a little, stop him with "Whoa" and a pull on the reins (a gentle pull-and-slack, pull-and-slack is more effective than a steady or harsh pull). He should stop readily, for both of these commands—your voice, and the pull on the reins—should be familiar to him from his driving lessons. Repeat this several times until he moves out readily for you and then stops when you want him to.

More than likely the horse will never buck with you because he has confidence in you and you have already acquainted him with the use of the reins, carrying the saddle, and so forth. Usually a horse bucks from confusion—so many new and strange things are done to him all at once!—or from irritation. By preparing for the first ride in gradual steps, and getting him accustomed to all the various equipment (and making sure it *fits* properly) and commands, you should have done away with the confusion and irritation. You are better off never to let him discover he can buck with you on his back.

It is very important that you don't overdo these first lessons. Five or ten minutes each to start with is plenty. Unsaddle him, talk to him, and perhaps give him a little grain before you turn him loose. This riding business is something new to him and you'll have much better luck with your training progress if you go slow, taking him along little by little so he will be attentive and learning throughout each lesson. You don't want him to become sour or rebellious.

Once you have started riding him, ride him *every* day, even twice or three times a day, just so long as each lesson is kept very brief. It is important to ride him often for the first few weeks, to keep him coming along readily, but just keep your actual riding time short. This is when the amateur trainer may get discouraged. You've been feeding and working with that young horse for two or three years and now you spend more time saddling and unsaddling him than riding him. But you are laying some very important groundwork for his later training, and it's best to go slow at this point. Remember also that he is still young and immature; too much riding at this point might do permanent damage to immature bones and tendons. Give him lots of short lessons on mounting and dismounting, and short rides around the corral.

As you begin working on his turning, it helps to use the fence a little in the early stages. As he comes to the fence, encourage him to turn one way or the other by use of your reins and legs, and if he begins to turn of his own accord, encourage the turn so that he will begin to associate your signals with turning; help him along. Use gentle leg pressure on the side away from which you want him to turn—he will tend to turn away from the leg pressure. Use your hands low on the reins, with a rein in each hand. If at times he doesn't want to turn, *don't* jerk him around. At this stage you don't need 100 percent correct response from him; he is learning many things besides reining, and it all takes time.

Spend most of the early sessions at the walk, then progress to an occasional trot. Don't rush him into a canter, because he's not ready for it until he has learned a great deal of control, and because you are still working in a fairly confined area. Don't prolong any lesson. Quit when he is working well, and don't continue to the point where he is tired and uncooperative.

After several lessons he should be turning and stopping for you fairly well, and you can ride him out into the open. It's best to ride him alone for the first dozen times or more so that he won't get the idea that another horse must be with him before he can leave the corral. After he gets used to the presence of another horse going along with him you can ride side by side. It's also good to let the other horse lead and follow a few times, so that your young horse will get used to the idea that the whereabouts of the other horse doesn't matter, and that his main job is to obey your signals and go where and at what pace you indicate, rather than having to follow another horse.

After you are riding him freely out in the open, you can work more and more on teaching him a fast walk and to respond better to your reining. You will probably ride miles and miles at the walk to develop his legs and his agility and balance with a rider on his back. And in

Starting Nikki as a three-year-old. Note the halter under the headstall and the use of reins attached to the halter as well as the snaffle reins. A halter can be used for a time on an overly ambitious horse, so that he can be checked partly with the halter as well as the bit (so that all the pressure isn't on his tender mouth).

Starting Khamette as a three-year-old, no longer needing the halter—working well in the snaffle bit.

all this traveling you can teach him a fast walk and start teaching him lightness and collection and a responsive mouth.

Some horses become overeager at some phase of their early training, and since you are probably riding in a snaffle bit you won't want to be constantly pulling or fussing with the horse's mouth, as this can tend to make him hard-mouthed and unresponsive. If your horse comes to a stage in which he is always trying to go a little faster than he should (and many high-spirited horses will), you can ride him with a close-fitting halter under the headstall with reins of some sort attached, so that if you must check him strongly or continually (if he is over-ambitious), you can put some pressure on the halter rather than all in his mouth. After he learns to go at the speed *you* want him to, you can dispense with the halter and extra reins.

While you are in these early stages of the horse's training under saddle will be a good time to teach him a fast walk. Some amateur trainers neglect this phase of a horse's training, and it is common to see many horses, even fairly well-trained horses, that poke along at the walk. The walk is an important gait, whether you are trail riding, in the show ring, riding range, or riding just for pleasure. A brisk, free-moving walk is much more pleasant than a plodding gait, and can make the difference of several miles of ground covered when you are riding. Some horses are naturally fast walkers, others are not. But with a little time and patience, any horse can be taught to walk fast.

When you start thinking about improving your horse's walk, you must consider that he should take longer strides, not just short fast choppy steps. Every time he pushes off with a longer swing of his leg, he will cover the ground faster, yet seem relaxed and unhurried.

The walk is a four-beat gait with this sequence: starting with the right hind leg, the next leg to move forward will be the right front, then the left hind, then the left front. You will want to stimulate your horse into moving his hind legs more energetically, to take longer strides. The only time you can stimulate your horse into moving a certain leg more energetically is at the instant it prepares to push off and swing through the air. After the leg is in the air you are too late with any urging because there is nothing the horse can do in response. So you will have to use your own legs to urge him at the proper time—your right leg as he gets ready to push off with his right hind, your left leg as he prepares to push off with his left hind, and so forth. His left front leg comes forward just ahead of the right hind, so if you are going to catch him before he pushes off with his right hind, you'd best use your own right leg as his left front foot hits the ground, or you will be too late.

The simplest way to do this is by watching his shoulder. As the left shoulder moves forward, you know his left front leg is in the air. As the left front foot grounds, squeeze with your right leg. Then as the right shoulder goes forward and the right front foot grounds, squeeze your left. Use your legs where they hang in the stirrups, not back toward the flank. And don't kick; a squeeze with the calves of your legs is better.

Lightly finger the reins to check him if he starts to break into a trot. Watching his shoulders to get the exact second, squeeze your own legs alternately. Try to feel the point at which he wants to break into a trot, and check him before he breaks gait. Each time you have to check him, immediately squeeze with your legs, urging him to walk faster instead of trotting.

After you get the feel of it, you'll be able to squeeze your legs alternately at the proper time without watching the horse's shoulder, for this comes naturally with the rhythm of the horse's movement at the walk. Squeezing your legs alternately at the proper time is much more effective in producing a fast walk than squeezing both legs together, and is also less tiring to you, for as you get the feel of it your legs will move almost naturally with the sway of the horse's body.

As you ride the horse more and more you can work on his reining, using the neck rein more all the time in preparation for when you will use the neck rein alone. At first you should change directions only slightly, but as he improves and understands the signals for turning, you can rein him at a more acute angle until you can readily turn him at a 90-degree angle. Use your legs and body in turning; he will catch on much faster. His natural tendency is to move away from leg pressure and to move in the direction you lean in order to restore proper balance. So when you want him to turn to the right, lean slightly to the right and press with your left leg. Usually gentle pressure is enough, but occasionally you may need to "boot" him around a turn if for some reason he doesn't want to go that direction. You will get almost 100 percent better response if you use legs as an aid in turning rather than trying to turn him with reins alone. With legs, he will turn with his whole body. Some horses that are just reined around a turn get "limber-necked," turning their heads but continuing straight ahead with their bodies. Using leg pressure will prevent this problem.

Push the horse into a free trot every now and then, but don't let him merely jog. Gradually push the trot until after a dozen lessons or so he is trotting his best. A lot of horses don't know how to do a brisk, free-moving trot under saddle because their riders have just let them jog all their lives.

It's all right to do a short free gallop occasionally so that the horse won't get the idea that he is never supposed to gallop with a rider on his back. But be sure you have him under control and the situation well in hand at all times. He may be inclined to buck playfully the way he does when running loose in the pasture, and you don't want him to do this with a rider on his back. This doesn't mean that you have to restrain him in any way while he gallops, just ride with a short rein so that you could easily check him if you have to.

Don't expect your horse to become well trained if you try to make him do things he is not ready for. While he is in this uncertain stage of being trained, don't ever race him or try games on horseback or attempt fast reining or sliding stops before he is ready for such things. It's fine to ride him with other horses in an ordinary manner while you are training him, but wait until he is thoroughly trained before you try fast work or enter contests with him. A month's work and training can be completely ruined by a few minutes of the wrong kind of riding.

And don't have anyone else ride him while you are training him if you ever plan to finish him. The green horse can be easily confused by anyone who uses his hands, legs, and weight in a different manner than you do. No two people ride alike. The other person may be an exceptionally fine rider and trainer, but if you are the one who is to finish the training of the horse, you should be the only one to ride him during his training period, for best results.

13

BITS AND THEIR USES

For many hundreds of years, the best way to control and communicate the rider's wishes to the horse has been through the control of the horse's mouth with a bit. We do not know exactly when men in ancient times stopped eating horses and began riding them, but pictures drawn as early as 2000 B.C. show men mounted on horses. By the seventh century B.C. the Assyrians were using bridles that were not too different from bridles we use today. The earliest writing about bridles and bits that we can find seems to have been written about the fifth century B.C. by the Greeks. The snaffle was the first bit developed, and was used on chariot horses.

In this chapter we will look briefly at the various types of bits in use today. The type of bit is not nearly so important as the horsemanship that accompanies it. There is no substitute for light hands, good seat and balance, and tact when it comes to developing or keeping a good mouth on a horse. By good mouth, I mean a mouth that is pliable and responsive to the bit. It has been said that any rider who is capable of using a severe bit on a horse doesn't need one, and anyone else should never use one. There is a lot of truth in that statement. But the factor that determines whether a bit is severe or mild is ultimately the horsemanship that accompanies it. The snaffle is called a gentle bit, but if there are rough hands behind it, even the snaffle can be a cruel bit.

There are basically only three types of bits, the snaffle, the curb, and the pelham (which is a combination of the snaffle and curb). Let's look first at the snaffles. Snaffles are mainly of two kinds, the straight bar or the jointed. The straight bar puts pressure straight back, directly on the corners of the mouth. The jointed snaffle comes back farther and can pinch if not used properly. It is more severe than the straight snaffle. A curved, unjointed snaffle, called a half moon, is the mildest type of snaffle bit, even milder than the straight snaffle, for the tongue of the horse has more room to move around.

156

The snaffle bit has a ring at each side of the mouthpiece for attaching to the cheek pieces of the headstall; this same ring is often used for attaching the reins. The snaffle bit has no leverage action; it restrains the horse by pressing on the bars and tongue and by direct movements to the side. There are many, many different kinds of snaffle mouthpieces in use today.

A good snaffle should have a fairly thick mouthpiece. A thin mouthpiece can cut or pinch the corners of the horse's mouth. A mild, thick snaffle is best when starting a young horse. No matter what style of bit you wish to use on the horse later, at first the horse should be started in a mild snaffle. You want the young horse to learn to move out boldly; with a mild bit and a thick mouthpiece the horse will be more likely to take hold of the bit without fear of it pinching or hurting him. The purpose of a bit is to communicate with the horse. But communication cannot be established if the horse is afraid or confused by the bit. A good snaffle for training is the "egg butt" snaffle—the ends of the mouthpiece are joined to the rings in a smooth meshing and will not pinch the horse's mouth.

The bit you use, whether snaffle, curb or pelham, must fit the horse. A bit that is too wide moves back and forth and is annoying to the horse. Narrow bits are even worse because they pinch and can make sores, or cause the horse to toss his head.

The mouthpiece of the bit should lie in the area between the incisors and the molars where there are no teeth. This area is very sensitive. The bars of the mouth where the bit rests are sharp-edged bones (the inside branches of the jawbone) with a thin covering of delicate skin and nerve endings. Rough use of a bit can damage these nerves permanently. The horse's tongue is sensitive, too, but it can move around and displace some discomfort caused by a bit that fits improperly or is used harshly. But the lips, bars, and chin groove cannot move about and escape the discomfort, so the horse may resort to tossing his head, pulling against the bit, and so forth. If a horse reacts adversely to a certain bit, the rider's first thought is to change bits and try something else. Sometimes this is the proper thing to do, because the bit must fit the horse to be comfortable to him. But all too often the rider goes to a more severe bit instead of trying to get a bit that fits properly, and this usually aggravates the horse's problem, especially if the problem was caused by the rider's rough hands to begin with.

Good hands are most important, but proper fit should never be neglected. Many years ago there was an instrument that horsemen used to measure horse's mouths. The exact dimensions of a horse's mouth were measured and then a bit was made especially to fit the horse. But today many bits are bought with no thought to their size or to the width of the mouth they are to fit. Too many bits are selected for other reasons than proper fit—cost, looks, a favorite style, or because a friend has one that works well on *his* horse. Some horse owners don't realize that bits and mouths differ, that different bits have different purposes, and that the horse's training and the rider's ability should be part of the determining factors in choosing a bit that is suitable for the horse.

Besides fitting properly, a bit should be balanced. This is very important. A balanced bit hangs properly in the horse's mouth, puts no unnecessary pressure on any one point, and is more comfortable to the horse (to say nothing of being more effective in training and riding). Balance is especially important in a curb or pelham. An unbalanced bit doesn't hang properly in the horse's mouth, the lower shanks may come forward when the horse mouths or feels the bit, and the points of contact in the horse's mouth are somewhat altered. In other words, you will not get proper action with a bit that is not balanced, and your horse may not work quite as well as he might in a properly balanced bit.

Many horses seem to like a heavy bit. The horses I have trained all seem to prefer and to work best in a bit made of a heavy metal (steel rather than aluminum, for instance). A horse seems to like the feel of it, and if it hangs properly it helps to set his head. The heavier the bit and reins, the lighter can be your touch on the reins. The horse can feel even the slightest motion of your fingers even if there is some slack in the reins, for the weight of the bit and reins keeps a light feel on his mouth at all times. A very light bit and light reins can't convey the same touch without a stronger fingering of the reins. In order to keep proper feel of the mouth with light reins, you give the impression of a "tight" rein. A heavy rein can keep the same touch and still have a little slack in it.

Now let's back up a little and look at the bits we use in training the young horse. As mentioned before, it is best to start a horse in a snaffle, for when used properly the snaffle is a mild bit that the horse will soon learn to accept and to work in. A horse must learn to accept the pressure of a bit without fear. He must learn to relax, flex, and be pliable to the rider's hands. If you as his trainer are able to develop a good mouth, he will not have a rigid head or neck. A horse that has a relaxed jaw can accept communication from the bit, for he is not afraid of his mouth. This is important in the training of any horse, be he a pleasure horse, jumper, or stock horse. Proper bitting and a good mouth are necessary before a horse can be light and "collected" and able to perform under saddle as he should. I'll discuss this in more detail in Chapter 15. The importance of a snaffle as a bit to start a young horse cannot be overemphasized. Because of its action, the purpose of the snaffle is to raise the head. An untrained horse is uncollected and heavy on his front end.

Until the horse learns to be collected and to travel light on his forehand (working with his hocks well under him), he should be kept on the snaffle. Then after he becomes light and collected he can be put into a curb bit.

When the horse is working well in the snaffle and is ready to be put into the curb, the transfer from snaffle to curb can be accomplished by use of a double bridle or pelham, or with a converter strap, or with a very short-shanked jointed curb, or with a training curb that has a jointed mouthpiece and rings for snaffle reins. The last two bits mentioned are often mistakenly called snaffles (such as "western snaffle" or "colt training snaffle"), but they have shanks and curb straps and are definitely in the family of curb bits.

A converter strap is a strap that attaches to both the snaffle and curb rings on a curb bit that has rings for both, and the reins are then attached to the converter strap. This way the reins put some pressure on the curb, but the horse can be "plow" reined if necessary. After the horse is ridden with the converter strap awhile it can be removed and he can be ridden in the curb bit.

I like to use a pelham to gradually work the horse into the curb from

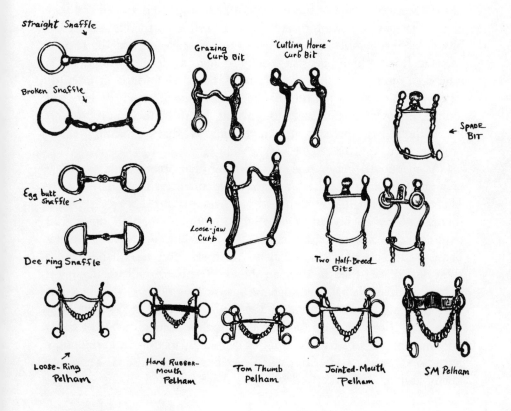

Straight Snaffle

Broken Snaffle

Egg butt Snaffle

Dee ring Snaffle

Grazing Curb Bit

"Cutting Horse" Curb Bit

A Loose-jaw Curb

SPADE BIT

Two Half-Breed Bits

Loose-Ring Pelham

Hard Rubber-Mouth Pelham

Tom Thumb Pelham

Jointed-Mouth Pelham

SM Pelham

the snaffle. At first I use only snaffle reins until the horse gets used to the bit. Then I put on the curb reins, too, and gradually use the curb reins more and the snaffle reins less as the horse learns to work in the curb. This takes several weeks. I like a pelham for gradually putting the horse into the curb, and also for setting the horse's head and further working on collecting him. The snaffle can be used to raise his head, and the curb reins can be used to tuck his nose in.

The curb bit has shanks, unlike the snaffle, and produces leverage action—putting pressure on the bars (or on the bars and tongue, depending on the bit). There are many types and styles of curb bit but they all work on the same principle. There are English curbs and western curbs. The English curb usually has a straight shank whereas the western curb's shanks curve backward. This curving is to prevent the horse's "lipping" the shanks. English curbs prevent this by use of a lip strap.

Here are a few main types of curb bits; you'll find many variations of each type. The grazing curb is a mild bit with a low port and short shank, short enough so that the horse can graze with this bit in his mouth. The "cutting horse bit" has a low port and long shanks, but is fairly mild because the shanks curve back instead of being straight, producing less leverage than a straight-shanked bit. The broken-mouth curb is often called a western snaffle or training bit; the mouthpiece is jointed and may or may not have a place for snaffle reins as well as curb reins. The "half-breed" bit is a combination of features in the spade bit and the regular curb bit. It has a high port that usually contains a cricket or roller, and is a bit used mostly on horses that are already well along in their training. The spade bit acts on the roof of the mouth as well as on the bars and tongue. A novice should never use this bit. It can be used on a properly trained horse by a master reinsman who knows what he is doing. If improperly used, this bit can be very severe.

As mentioned before, the horsemanship that accompanies the bit is of utmost importance. The bit is not as important as the horsemanship. Many riders seem to think that bits are for making horses do certain things; the novice horseman usually places more emphasis on the bit than does the experienced horseman. The good horseman puts more emphasis on the use of his legs, balance, firm seat and good hands, and a great deal of tact than he does on the bit. The horse will usually resort to some undesirable habit as a defense against rough hands—head tossing, tongue rolling, mouth opening, and so forth—and once he develops these habits it is hard to get rid of them even with a change of bits or better horsemanship. It's best to use a lot of care and patience while training a horse so that these bad habits will never become established. There is a saying that he who travels slowly gets there first, and this is very true of training horses. Take a close look at yourself and your horsemanship and the methods you want to use in training your horse. Don't blame the horse if he makes mistakes or seems rebellious; this is the fault of the trainer, not the horse. If you are not getting the desired results with your horse, take a closer look at your own horsemanship, the use of your hands, and the training methods you are using.

14

HOW THE HORSE MOVES

Knowing some of the facts about how a horse moves can be a help in becoming a better horseman, trainer, or judge of horses. A working knowledge of the anatomy and athletic ability of the horse and how he functions at the various gaits shows us the "why" of good horsemanship; if we know something about the horse's gaits and how he moves, it's easier to understand how and when to use certain aids to make the horse do what we want him to. This knowledge also enables us to use good judgment in what we ask of the horse—not asking him to do something that is physically beyond his ability in a given circumstance.

The horse has strong muscles in the upper part of each leg. But below the knees and hocks there are no muscles; the muscles from the upper leg continue downward as tendons. The muscles in the front of the forearm pull the lower leg forward (extend it), and help in "pulling" the body along when the horse is in motion. The muscles at the back of the forearm bend the knee.

A long forearm allows for longer muscles and shorter tendons. This is why many horsemen look for short cannons in a horse. There will be more length of muscle (therefore more speed and endurance—long muscle produces more speed and endurance than short, thick muscle) above the knee than in a horse with a short forearm.

The horse's center of gravity lies right behind his withers; his front end, with head and neck, is heavier than his hindquarters. Most of his weight is carried by his front legs. A horse that is standing squarely on all four feet can't lift a front foot until he raises his head and crouches a little on his hind legs or moves a hind leg forward to take more of the weight. You've probably noticed this fact if you have ever started to lead a horse that has been standing squarely. If you didn't have any slack in the rope as you moved forward, he probably pulled you back a couple of

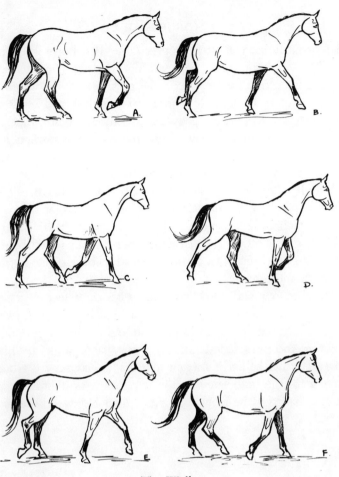

The Walk.

inches when he raised his head and shifted his weight to the rear in order to move a front foot.

To move in any direction, the horse has to overcome the fact that he is front-heavy. This is why he must be "collected" in order to move well-balanced—with his head up, his chin tucked in, and his weight carried further back so he is "light" on his front end.

When a horse walks, he brings each leg forward at the exact moment to keep himself balanced. He crouches slightly as he takes extra weight on his hind feet in order to move a front foot forward. He uses his head and neck for balance, just as we swing our arms when we walk or run. At the walk and at the canter and gallop the horse's head bobs at each step. His head drops each time a front foot comes to the ground, and his hip drops each time a hind foot comes to the ground.

By watching the horse's head or hip, you can tell which front foot or hind foot he limps with if he is ever lame. If a horse is lame in the left front foot, for instance, his head will drop farther when his right foot (his good foot) comes to the ground; he tries to keep his weight off his lame foot, therefore he takes a shorter stride with it and tends to keep his head up, trying to pull his body along without landing much weight on it. He lets his head bob down with more emphasis when his good foot lands.

The horse makes balancing movements with his head and neck at the walk and gallop but not at the trot because his balance is steadier at the trot. When he trots, his body is supported on diagonal legs at each stride (right front and left hind, or left front and right hind). The trot is a two-beat gait. Thus at each stride the horse is supported by a leg on each side and at each end of his body, instead of by just one leg or three as in the walk and canter.

During the slow walk the horse usually has three feet on the ground at once and moves one leg at a time. As a hind leg comes forward, the front foot on that side prepares to push off and leaves the ground a split second before the hind foot lands. At a very slow walk the hind foot lands several inches behind the front foot that is leaving the ground, but at a faster walk the hind lands in the same track or a little in advance of the track made by the front foot. At a good fast walk, the hind foot

The horse shifts his weight to the hind feet as he comes to a sudden stop. To do this, he raises his head, crouches down on his hindquarters, and slides his hind legs under him.

of most horses will land well in advance of the track made by the front foot that has just been picked up—ten or twelve inches or even more. A horse that makes long strides with his hind feet (greatly overstepping the tracks made by the front feet) will be able to walk faster and farther without tiring than a horse that makes short choppy strides.

When the horse is asked to stop, the momentum of his body is still moving him forward, so he uses his front heels as brakes while he straightens out his front legs and shifts his weight to the rear by planting his hind feet on the ground in front of their normal standing position. He does this by raising his head, and flexing his hocks and stifles—crouching at the rear a little to shift his weight to his hind feet and thus come to a stop.

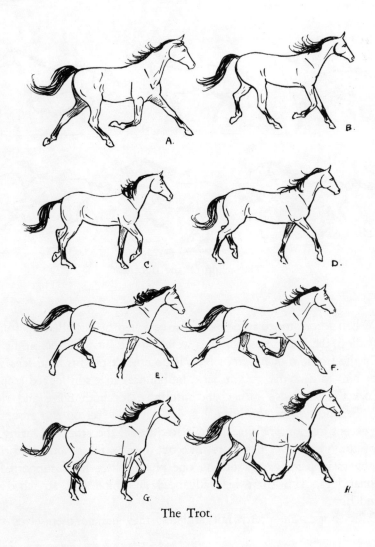

The Trot.

The gallop on the right lead.

When forced to stop unexpectedly, or when he is pulled up from a fast gallop, the horse must shift his weight to his hind feet before he can regain the freedom of his front feet. If he doesn't put his hind legs well under him to shift the weight back, he bounces to a stiff-legged stop on his locked front legs—rather uncomfortable for both horse and rider.

When he canters, the horse has one or three feet on the ground at once except for the time that all four feet are off the ground. During the gallop the horse never has more than two feet on the ground, and these are always in pairs, except during one phase where he is supported by diagonal legs, with front legs advanced and hind legs stretched out behind him.

Most horses are pretty fair athletes; they handle themselves with

The canter on the right lead.

agility, dexterity, and good balance when they are running free in a pasture or in the hills on the range. There are exceptions, of course. Some horses are more clumsy than others. But a lot of horses that are good athletes when running loose do not handle themselves as well with a rider on their back (especially young horses in training). This is partly because the added weight of the rider makes the balance different, and also because the horse does not always know exactly what's going to happen next and isn't always prepared for a sudden stop or change of direction or some other maneuver the rider asks of him. He may be at the wrong phase of a stride to execute the new maneuver immediately or properly. This is why a rider, and especially a trainer, needs to know something about the way the horse moves, so that he can give his horse the proper signals at the proper time.

This is also why a horse needs a lot of work and training at all gaits in order to develop dexterity and balance with a rider on his back, and gain the ability to adjust his stride to the situation. Experience improves the ability of both the horse and the rider. The horse learns to travel well with a rider on his back, and the rider learns (we hope) how to collect the horse and how to give the proper signals at the proper time for best response from the horse.

15

TEACHING LIGHTNESS AND COLLECTION

An earlier chapter dealt with starting the young horse under saddle. Now I'd like to cover some of the next steps in his training. For the first few weeks of the horse's training he has been traveling in an extended manner; he is not "collected." In other words, his hind feet are not well under him, his head and neck are fairly low, and he travels heavy on his front end.

Teaching a horse to be light and collected is one of the most important aspects of his training. He can't perform at his best until he is collected, with his weight balanced farther back to free his front end for whatever new movement the rider asks of him. Training a horse to be light on his front end may take a lot of time. It's not something that should be done in a hurry. You should begin at the walk and trot and not go any further until you are sure he is collected at these gaits. After a horse is completely trained, you can let him travel in an extended manner sometimes on long rides, but when there is work to be done or a precise action wanted, the horse must be collected.

When a horse is collected, his head is above the level, his neck is slightly arched and flexed at the poll so that his nose is down, chin tucked in, and forehead almost perpendicular to the ground. His lower jaw is relaxed and responsive to the light hands of the rider. His hind feet are well under his body and he is balanced and ready for movement in any direction.

A horse balances himself by raising or lowering his head and changing the position of his hind feet. The lower his head, the harder it is for him to move freely, for the heavier he is on his front end; he is not prepared for sudden movement. To move freely, he must be able to get the weight off his front feet, to free his front feet for action. In order to be light on his feet and prepared for sudden changes of direction, the horse

Collected (top), Extended (bottom).

must have his head up and his weight balanced back on his hind feet.

For this reason you can see that the popular notion that a cutting horse must have his head low when he works cattle is incorrect. Of course the head of a stock horse should not be *too* high, but it should still be level with the rest of his body or higher where it doesn't interfere with his balance. When his head is low it takes a great effort for the horse to bring his hind feet forward far enough for executing quick stops and changes of direction.

You've probably noticed the difference in how a green horse handles himself with a rider on his back and how a trained stock horse handles himself (or any well-trained horse, for that matter). The stock horse is ready to spring into action at any time. From a walk or a standstill he can leap into action in any direction you indicate in order to turn a cow. But the green horse is slow when you need to turn a cow; in fact, he's almost awkward—as if he were rooted to the ground or as if his legs don't function properly. He may understand the signals you give him and try to move out as you indicate, but he is not collected. His legs are not under him properly and he is not in the right position with the right balance for a well-controlled turn, fast start or quick stop. He must learn to be collected before he can become well-coordinated with you on his back and ready to instantly respond in the proper degree to your signals, without your having to force him. I have seen riders try to make their horses do things beyond their ability, and this results in kicking the horse

If the horse is collected and balanced, he can turn quickly and easily.

around, jerking him around, jerking him to a stop, etc. The horse should not be forced to execute fast movements until he is far along enough in his training to be ready for them.

Setting of the horse's head when teaching him collection is done by proper use of the bit with light hands. If you often finger the reins (using a snaffle bit) lightly when you are training your horse, he will tend to raise his head. Early training in a bit should be done with a snaffle. After the horse is trained he will perform well in almost any kind of bit that fits him if you have light hands, but early training should be done with the snaffle.

When you begin to teach the horse collection, start using your legs more strongly. This makes the horse push his hind legs farther under himself as he does when he is moving faster. But instead of letting him move faster or break into a faster gait, you finger the reins lightly to keep him at the slower gait. It takes good judgement and lots of practice to know just how much bit and how much legs to use (how much bit pressure and how much leg pressure), but as you practice the horse should gradually raise his head and flex his neck, balancing his weight farther back and gathering himself with hind feet well under him. He will then be traveling with his chin tucked in and his lower jaw relaxed and not tense against the bit. If he is merely traveling with chin tucked in and his mouth *behind* the bit, you have not succeeded in collecting him—you've probably been too forceful with the bit. When a horse is collected his jaw is soft and pliable to the bit, he is "on" the bit and ready to respond to any movement of your hands. It takes a delicate touch.

Producing lightness and collection in a horse is the essence of good training. Everything you teach your horse after his first elementary lessons (bridling, saddling, mounting, moving out, etc.) is aimed at making him more pleasant to ride and more able to perform the actions that you will want him to do. You want him light in your hands and agile, and able to adjust his stride to the situation. Young horses, and many mature horses that haven't been properly trained, have not developed this ability. Most young horses, no matter how agile and graceful they are running free, are awkward with a rider on their back. It's up to you as trainer to develop your horse's natural ability to its fullest potential.

Training a horse to be collected should be done only at the walk at first, and then at the trot after the walk has been mastered. A collected walk is not necessarily a slow walk. Some horses are naturally eager walkers, but many horses do not learn to walk fast until they learn collection. To get a collected walk, urge your horse with your legs, but finger the bit enough to keep him from breaking into a trot. His energy will be "bottled up," so to speak, and will have to come forth as a faster, more animated walk instead of a trot.

By proper judgement as to how much bit and how much leg you use, you can do either a slow collected walk or a fast collected walk. All the horses I have trained seem to walk much better when they are collected, so I teach them collection in order to teach them a fast walk. It helps to use your legs alternately when urging the horse to a fast walk, squeezing in rhythm with the horse, as explained earlier in chapter twelve.

Most horses do a good trot naturally. If you have pushed the horse to a good fast trot in his early training, it is easy to make him do a collected trot when you start working on making him light. Slow the horse from a fast trot, using your legs sufficiently to keep him from coming to a walk. There is a lot of difference between a slow trot and a collected trot. Most horses merely plod along at the slow trot or "jog," barely picking up their feet and looking as though they might fall apart or fall down at any step. A collected trot is much more animated. In order to get a collected trot, keep fingering the reins to keep the horse slow, but continue to use your legs a little to keep him lightly on the bit and well gathered.

Teaching the horse two speeds at the trot makes him more agile and develops his ability to lengthen and shorten his stride. The slowing down is also good in teaching the horse to respond to the increased feel of the bit on the bars of his mouth. Many horses carry too much of their weight on their front legs (travel too heavily on their forehand) when ridden, and this exercise in slowing down, especially when done abruptly —as you will do in later stages of training—is good to lighten his forehand. When slowing down, especially abruptly, his weight comes off his forehand and back toward his quarters. He will need to learn this to be able to do a good stop later on, or to distribute his weight off his front legs for a fast turn or pivot on his hind legs.

Your hands control the horse's forehand, in slowing him, collecting him, indicating direction, etc., and your legs control his hindquarters in turning, pushing his hind legs farther under him, urging him faster, and so forth. Your legs are very important in turning; they aid in turning the whole horse, not just the neck, and help to make a smooth turn.

You want the horse to turn smoothly and easily and he can do this only if he is balanced and collected. Otherwise he may turn awkwardly on his front legs instead of turning on his hind legs. In later stages of training you may want your horse to be able to pivot on his hind legs and spin around to change directions quickly, so it's a good idea to give him some background training for this, getting him collected and using your legs when you turn, teaching him to shift his weight back and turn on his hind legs.

When you teach your horse to pivot on his hind legs, you'll want his front end to swing around while his hindquarters stay in place. You use your legs to hold his hindquarters in place while you rein his front end around. When starting to teach your horse to turn on his haunches this way, don't expect him to turn on a very large angle at first; just ask him for one step at a time. Sometimes it helps to halt him parallel to a fence. With the fence on one side he will more readily turn away from it. He will understand your signal to turn in that direction because he can see very well that he can't turn the other direction—into the fence.

Use your legs to urge him to make a step, but use your hands to rein him so that he will make the step to the left, let's say, instead of forward. Check him just enough so that he will move his front legs but not his hind legs. Some horses will want to move their hindquarters to the side instead of their front legs because this is easier for them to do. Remember that when standing, the horse normally carries most of his weight on his front legs; this is why you must teach the horse collection and the ability to shift more weight to his hind feet to lighten his forehand so he can move his front legs more easily. The horse will also catch on faster to this business of pivoting on his hindquarters if you have taught him to turn on his haunches during the early training you did with him from the ground. When teaching him while you are mounted, use your inside leg to steady the hindquarters and your outside leg back behind the girth even more strongly to keep the hindquarters from swinging out as the horse turns.

When the horse begins to turn correctly, you should be able to make him pivot in a 180-degree turn in four distinct steps. Throughout the turn he should keep his body straight from poll to croup, not bending his head and neck around, etc. If he tries to pivot on his front legs instead of his hind legs, move your outside leg back farther and squeeze strongly or tap him with it to keep his hindquarters from swinging out.

After he has learned to pivot well, you can begin turning him this way from a walk, then from a trot, and finally from a canter. But remember that you must work him up to fast reining gradually. Don't rush him into something he is not ready for. Work him along a fence and he will catch on more easily. Always halt him before you give the signal to turn, and gather him back onto his hind feet before you turn him. If he doesn't have his hind feet well under him, he can't pick up his front feet and pivot around. It helps to lean a little in the direction of the turn. The more sudden and fast the turn, the more you should lean, and the more decisive should be your hand and leg action.

It takes time for your horse to learn to pivot quickly and well. Never rush him, and don't ever jerk his mouth or try to jerk him around. Before he can master the pivot on the hind legs, he must develop the ability to shift his weight back, come to a smooth stop, and be able to turn on his

Pivot on hind legs. Rider stops the horse, gathers him back on his hind legs, leans in the direction of the turn, reins him around, and uses his outside leg strongly to encourage the horse to pivot around.

hind legs. He can't do it if he travels heavy on his front end, so he must be collected.

Now let's back up a little and talk about teaching the horse to stop smoothly. This is part of teaching him collection and is a necessary step before he can learn to pivot well at any gait.

The horse is taught to stop smoothly and easily through repetition, reward, and punishment. He should know about stopping from the early training you did (driving, longeing, using the command "Whoa," etc.). When you are mounted and wish him to stop, lean back slightly, give him the command to stop, and check him lightly with the reins. If he stops, immediately release the tension on the reins and the feel on his mouth.

Thus he is rewarded for stopping by a release of pressure. If he doesn't stop, increase your checking with the reins until he does stop. It is better to use a series of "give and take" actions with the reins (or a vibrating of the bit by a series of short pulls) than a steady pull; the horse will pay more attention to it. Many horses that do not stop well have riders that never give them any "reward" or slack; the reins are always tight and the horse doesn't pay any attention to the signal to stop because the rider pulls all the time.

If you are satisfied with the stop you get from a walk, try a slow trot. When he stops well from a slow trot, try a fast trot. Then move on to the canter. If at any time he refuses to stop smoothly go back to a slower gait and work on his stop until he once again does it well from the slower gait. During your training sessions and in all your riding thereafter, try to avoid stopping the horse on rocky or uneven ground. Sometimes when you are chasing cattle in the mountains you can't avoid it, but there is no sense in causing the horse pain unnecessarily. A fast stop or turn on rocky ground will hurt his feet and he may be reluctant to do it again— he will associate the pain with stopping or turning.

I might add a word here about sliding stops. Sliding stops may be spectacular in the show ring, but they are very impractical anywhere else (and even impractical in the show ring if you are going to ask the horse to do a fast turn after he stops). In the mountains or on rough ground, a sliding stop is very hard on the horse's legs, for reasons that should be

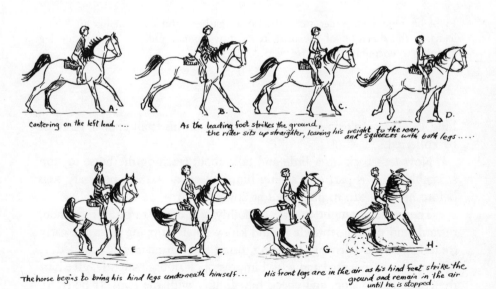

Cantering on the left lead. ...

As the leading foot strikes the ground, the rider sits up straighter, leaning his weight to the rear, and squeezes with both legs .....

The horse begins to bring his hind legs underneath himself...

His front legs are in the air as his hind feet strike the ground and remain in the air until he is stopped.

For a smooth, well-balanced stop . . .

quite obvious. Another factor to be considered, no matter where you are working the horse, is his balance. The purpose of the fast stop is for the horse to stop as quickly as possible without discomfort to himself or his rider, *not* how far he can slide. It is important that the horse stop in a balanced position so that if the rider asks him to make a quick turn, the horse can execute the turn right away. If his hind legs are locked under him in a long sliding stop, he will have to regain his balance before he can make a turn. A horse should stop on his hind feet, but he doesn't need to slide much. A well-trained horse can stop in less than five feet from racing speed if he is properly collected and balanced.

Let's look at how we get a balanced stop from a canter or gallop. Timing is important. If you ask the horse to stop at the wrong phase of his stride, his hind legs would not be in the right position for him to stop properly, and the result would be a series of jarring hops on his front legs with all his weight on his front end. You must ask him to stop as his hind legs are coming forward under him, *not* when they are extended backward completing their drive.

To get the idea, canter the horse slowly, feeling the rhythm of his movement and watching the lead foot as it strikes the ground. Time yourself to this rhythm. You want to ask the horse to stop when the lead foot strikes the ground, for this is the time the hind legs are starting to come forward for another stride. To ask the horse to stop, sit up straighter in the saddle and lean back a little as you check him slightly with the reins, raising his head a little without really pulling on the reins. By raising his head you help him raise his forehand and clear the ground with his front feet as he makes the stop. Sometimes it helps to squeeze with your legs a little as you ask for the stop and lean back, causing the horse to drive his hind legs underneath himself. But if you do this you will have to check him adequately at the same time so that he will stop instead of increasing speed.

After the horse does a good stop from an easy canter, you can gradually increase speed to where he will do a smooth stop from a fast gallop. When the horse stops well-balanced, he should use his hind legs to stop, taking his weight on them under his body, but not *too* far under. He uses his hocks, stifle and hips to help cushion the stop, and keeps his front legs off the ground until he has stopped.

One aspect of training that hasn't been mentioned yet is teaching the horse to back up under saddle. Now might be a good time to cover this phase of his training. We have not discussed it earlier, for two reasons. Backing can sometimes be a frightening experience for a young, excitable horse, and you'll have better luck saving this phase of his training until after he is well along in other areas. Also, if you save backing until after he has learned several other maneuvers, he won't be so inclined to back up when he is confused while being introduced to a new movement he doesn't yet understand (for instance in teaching him to rotate on forehand or quarters, or to walk on two tracks, side step, etc.). When a horse is asked to do a new exercise that is a little difficult for him to grasp, he usually tries to please the rider by performing another maneuver that he has already learned, and this is usually the back-up. By saving the backing until later in his training, you won't be so bothered by this.

Backing a horse looks simple when it is done well, but it can be a little tricky. When a horse backs calmly and well, it is as if he were trotting, as far as the way his legs work; the legs move together in diagonal pairs. His head and neck are somewhat extended and his mouth is closed. His movement will be relaxed, smooth, and straight. Many horses do not back well, and move one leg at a time, or have jaw set or mouth open. Their backing is usually crooked. Or in another form of bad backing the horse may tuck his chin in, drop the bit, and rush backward.

The horse mainly uses his front legs to propel himself backward, not his hind legs. Many trainers use the same aids for backing as they do for stopping, but this is incorrect because in the stop most of the horse's weight is on his hindquarters whereas in backing most of the weight is on his front legs.

To teach the horse to back, halt him from a walk and wait until he is calm and relaxed. Sit in a balanced position, then put your weight in your stirrups, collecting the horse and flexing him slightly, getting his attention through light use of your legs and fingers. Then squeeze with your legs and lean back slightly to indicate the direction. Most of your weight should be on your knees and thighs. The horse will be impelled to move because of the leg pressure, but his movement will be backward because your hands will check all forward movement. But do not *pull* on the reins. Keep your hands fixed to resist the forward impulse of the horse, perhaps vibrating the bit a little in his mouth. As he begins the first step backward, slack the reins immediately and relax the pressure of your legs. He should be rewarded for his obedience by relaxing the aids so that he can relax and know he has done the proper thing. As soon as he completes the step backward, ask for another, repeating the process. Your hand is fixed in place and your legs push the horse into the bit. Since he can't go forward, he goes backward. After he has done about four good steps backward, walk him quietly forward. The first lessons should not be prolonged or overdone.

As he learns what is expected of him in backing, he should be able to back as long as you ask a backward step of him, and be ready to step forward again without halting if you apply leg pressure and release rein pressure.

If he begins to back crookedly or swings his hindquarters to one side, use your leg behind the girth on the side that is "bulging out" to urge him to move his hindquarters back to a straight line again. It also helps to increase the tension slightly of the rein on that same side. If the horse begins to rush backward, stop him between each step with your leg pressure and a release of tension on the bit. If you overdo this he will take it as a signal to go forward, so you must synchronize your hands and legs.

Never try to back the horse by jerking his mouth or pulling on him without the leg aids. This only confuses the horse. Instead of being pushed into the bit he will merely fight it, throwing his head in the air or bracing his neck. To teach the horse to back smoothly and willingly, you must reward him by relaxing the aids as he obeys. Otherwise he may just fight you, for he doesn't understand what you are trying to do.

Before ending this chapter, I should mention the side-step. To side-step to the right, use your left leg strongly to start the horse's hindquarters moving to the right, and finger the reins lightly to keep him from going forward. At the same time push his front end to the right with your indirect rein (left rein). You will want to use two hands on the reins until he has learned this movement, for you can use both the indirect and direct rein to encourage him to take a step sideways if need be. After he understands the movement he can be made to side-step with just the indirect rein and you will only need one hand on the reins. After he makes two or three steps to the side, release all pressure and let him relax. Repeat the process in the other direction so that he will learn to side-step both ways. In teaching the side-step, lean your body slightly in the direction you wish him to go; he will tend to move over that way to restore proper balance. When the horse has been taught to side-step, to rotate on his front legs and on his hindquarters, and to back up, you will find it possible to open a gate from his back, enter it, and close it again without ever dismounting.

Sometimes a horse will become "sour" while in training, from so much constant use of your legs. To avoid this, allow him on some days to extend himself and forget collection every now and then. We seldom have this problem when training horses here on the ranch, for we use the horses riding range and checking cattle and there is so much traveling to do that it takes up a much larger percentage of our riding time than does our concentration on any one aspect of schooling the horse. In many ways I think this is the best way to train a horse—using him in the actual work of the ranch and gradually doing more and more things with him as he becomes ready, taking time out here and there to introduce him to a new movement or exercise, usually after he has several miles under his belt and is "warmed up" and ready to pay attention to what you are asking of him. As he becomes more agile and well-balanced under saddle, he can begin to take part in more and more of the active chores of moving or sorting cattle. By the end of one summer's ranch use, a "green" horse is usually fairly well along in his schooling and quite a useful cowhorse, and, except for the more strenuous aspects of training and working cattle (which we won't ask of him until he is older), has mastered much of the basic maneuvers that every well-trained horse should be able to do.

One last word about the use of your legs in training the horse. The horse should respond energetically and calmly to your legs, and they shouldn't have to be used hard to get his response (whether it be in teaching him to rotate, or to side-step, or to walk faster, increase his stride, etc.). If the horse responds sluggishly when you use your legs softly, *don't* use them more and more strenuously; you are just nagging and won't do that much good. Instead, use a switch emphatically in back of your leg if he pays no attention to the pressure of your legs. The switch will call attention to the soft signal you gave with your legs, and after a while the horse will prefer to obey the soft signal instead of having to feel the whip. This puts teeth into your argument and backs up your command.

In training your horse, use good judgment in everything you ask the horse to do and don't command him to do anything too difficult. But after having given a command to do something that he *should* be able to do, be emphatic and get the horse's obedience. He will progress further in his training if he respects your commands and finds out that you are always consistent—reasonable in what you ask of him, and emphatic in demanding that he always obey what you do ask of him.

16

CANTERING AND PROPER LEADS

You can consider your horse fairly well along in his training after you and he have mastered collection at the canter and the ability to take either lead from a standstill and to change leads smoothly at your signal when cantering on the straightaway.

As trainer, you should be familiar with all the details of the canter and gallop, for these gaits bring out all your skill (or lack of it) as a rider and also demand good training and obedience on the horse's part to be accomplished smoothly and well. If you are familiar with the way the horse moves at these gaits, you can more readily understand how and when to use certain aids to make the horse perform as desired. When you wish to put your horse into a canter on a certain lead or make him change leads, you must consider the effect of your legs and reins. The horse must first be in such a position that leaves no room for hesitation or confusion; you must give the leg and rein signals at such a phase in his stride or put him in such a position that he is physically able to obey your signals.

The "canter" is a slow and collected gallop. There is a difference between a collected gallop and a slow gallop. I have seen horses in the show ring that, when asked to canter, were indeed slow enough, but lacked collection and animation and looked as though they were about to fall down at every stride. They traveled too heavily on their forehand and would not be able to change directions suddenly if they had to.

In the fast gallop there is a phase in each stride during which all four feet are in the air. At the fast gallop the feet strike the ground so nearly at the same time (so quickly) that the sound of the four hoofbeats blend together. When slowed down to a canter, the horse's feet strike the ground more slowly, producing a definite one-two-three beat.

When cantering, the horse has one or three feet on the ground at once except for the time when all four feet are off the ground (see the illustrations in Chapter 14). If the horse is leading with the legs on the right side, for instance, the left hind foot strikes the ground first for beat one, the right hind and left front strike in unison for beat two, and the right front leg strikes for beat three. When galloping, the horse never has more than two feet on the ground at once.

Cantering or galloping, a horse always leads with his right or left feet. When cantering in a circle to the left, the left legs come forward

The top horse is in the left lead. His right hind foot will come to the ground first, then his left hind leg will come to the ground and lead. His right front will strike the ground next, then his left front will come forward and lead.

The bottom horse is in the right lead. His leading hind foot is still on the ground and his right front foot has just come to the ground farther forward of his left front.

in advance of the right legs. In making a turn or a circle, the horse naturally leads with his "inside" legs to brace himself. A horse on the wrong lead when making a tight circle or a sharp turn is liable to fall down.

This is how the horse's legs work when he is in the left lead. The right hind foot strikes the ground first, the left hind reaches farther and comes to the ground in advance of the right. Then the right front foot lands, followed by the left front which reaches ahead and leads.

A horse cantering or galloping will either be in the left lead or the right lead, or be "disunited." The horse is disunited if he starts a gallop or canter on one lead in front and the opposite lead behind, producing a rolling motion of his body which is very uncomfortable to the rider and also dangerous. When a horse is disunited he might strike a front leg with a hind and throw himself or break a leg. If your horse ever starts on one lead in front and the opposite lead behind, stop him and start him over again.

When you are mounted there are several ways you can tell which legs your horse is leading with. If he is in the left lead, a glance down at his shoulders will show you that his left shoulder moves about four inches in advance of his right (in the right lead, his right shoulder will be ahead of his left). Also, your inside leg (left leg if the horse is in the left lead, right leg if he is in the right lead) will be in motion whereas your outside leg will be comparatively still. Some inexperienced riders lean over to look at the horse's front legs to tell which lead the horse is in, but this excessive leaning can throw the horse off balance.

When you start teaching the horse to canter, it is best, at first, to pay no attention to leads; let the horse lead as he chooses. If you try to concentrate on leads as well as on teaching the horse a collected canter, you may confuse him—that's too many things for him to think about all at once. Let's work on getting a nicely controlled canter first.

A horse responds to your shifting weight because this changes his center of gravity. When you lean farther forward he tends to go faster in order to restore his balance, and when you lean back, he tends to slow down for the same reason. To teach the horse a slow and collected canter, urge with your legs sufficiently to keep him cantering instead of trotting, and finger the reins constantly to keep him from going faster. You can use your weight direction to advantage here, sitting more upright than you would at the gallop. If you lean forward too much the horse will try to go faster. Using your weight farther back in a more upright position helps keep him collected. His head will be raised instead of extended, and his hind legs will push farther underneath his body; he will have more spring to his movements and be in a well-balanced position. His propelling power will be directed up and down as well as forward.

With practice the horse should soon be able to do a slow and collected canter. You should be able to put him into a canter from a walk or from a standstill by leaning forward, squeezing your legs strongly, and lifting the reins. As the horse takes the first cantering stride, you lean back slightly and then continue using legs and hands to keep him from speeding or slowing into a trot.

After he has learned to canter well you can begin teaching him to take the proper leads at your signals. Most horses take either lead easily when they are running free without a rider on their backs. But the added weight of the rider, plus the fact that the horse isn't sure what to expect next, makes most young horses very awkward at first, especially with their leads.

Most horses prefer to canter in the left lead when mounted, and many will not take the right lead until taught to do so. This is because most horses, like most people, are "right-handed." When a horse goes into a canter or gallop, he raises his front end and gives a push with his hind legs, most of the push coming from the hind leg on the side opposite the leg with which he intends to lead. Therefore, because he is "right-footed," his driving power comes from his right hind leg and he naturally goes into the left lead. At the same time he gives this push with his right hind leg, his muzzle will be slightly tilted upward to the left.

There are several ways to put a horse into a certain lead. One method may work well for one trainer and not for another. Or one individual horse may respond better to one method than another horse. One method may work well on most horses for you, but occasionally a problem horse might come along that you will want to try another method with.

When putting the horse into a canter on a certain lead (whether from a standstill, a walk, or a trot), most trainers agree that the rider should squeeze hardest with his "outside" leg—the leg opposite the side you wish the horse to lead. This stimulates the horse to give his greatest push with his outside hind leg and thus he will naturally lead with his inside legs. Also, the horse tends to move away from leg pressure, and will more naturally lead with his inside legs if you put him into a canter on a turn and squeeze with your outside leg.

Some trainers lean forward and to the inside, particularly if they are putting the horse into the canter on a turn or making a circle; their leaning to the inside (and using the reins to indicate the direction at the same time) help tell the horse which way to move and he will more readily lead with his inside legs as this is his natural tendency

Going into the canter on the right lead from a standstill (top). The rider
squeezes with his left leg, putting the horse into the canter from a trot at a turn
(bottom). To put him into the right lead, the rider leans a little into the turn
and squeezes with his outside leg.

when making a turn or a circle. Other trainers lean slightly back and
to the outside as they squeeze the outside leg, at the same time tilting
the horse's muzzle slightly up with the inside rein. This is because
the horse naturally tilts his muzzle slightly in the direction he will lead.
The trainer leans back and to the outside to take the weight off the
horse's leading legs and thus "free" them to lead. Whichever school
of thought you follow (whether you lean to the inside or to the outside
as you signal the horse to canter) will probably depend on the results
you get from the horse. Some horses take a lead more readily with the
first method; others respond better to the second. Whichever method
you use, it's best to lean only slightly, so as not to push the horse off
balance, and concentrate most on using your outside leg strongly. If you

are working in an arena or in an enclosure, it helps sometimes to turn
the horse's head toward the fence just before you give him the signal
to canter, angling him slightly into the fence. If he takes a step or two
at this angle he will be forced to lead with inside legs when you squeeze
with your outside leg and put him into the canter. After he has learned
to take his leads properly you won't have to do this.

If the horse breaks into the canter on the correct lead, let him continue, but if he takes the wrong lead, immediately slow him down to
a trot and start over. Never let him continue cantering in the wrong
lead or he won't learn to take the proper lead at your signal.

On a green horse it's usually easier to put him into a canter on the
correct lead from a trot, rather than trying to start out in a canter from
a walk or a standstill. After he learns your signals and develops better
coordination he will more readily take up the canter on either lead at
your signal from a walk or a standstill.

Another suggestion when starting to teach a horse his leads; give
him the signal to canter when going into a turn. Here you can take
advantage of his natural tendency to lead with his inside legs. Be sure
to make him take the right lead as often as the left and vice versa, so
he won't become a "one-lead horse." And give him the signal to canter
and take a specific lead at various places in the area where you are working
him so he won't anticipate your signals always at the same place.

When he is taking his leads well at your signals, you should be able
to put him into either lead on the straightaway as well as on a turn, and
into either lead from a standstill, walk, or trot. If at any time he becomes
confused or won't take a certain lead, go back to putting him into it on
a turn. After a while he will associate your signals with the proper lead
and he won't have to be making a turn to understand which lead to take.

When the horse takes the proper leads readily at your signal, you
can go a step further and teach him the change of leads at the canter.
This is also called the flying change of leads, for at the canter the
horse must change his leads during the split second that all four feet
are in the air. Horses change leads this way naturally but usually must
be taught to do it with a rider on their backs. Some horses will change
leads fine when chasing cattle, but usually must be taught to change
for arena work or any other riding in which the horse does not always
anticipate the change of directions that the rider calls for.

Many horses readily change leads in front, but not behind; others are
a few strides slow in changing behind. When changing leads properly
(as the horse does when running free) the horse should change his hind
lead first, then his front, for this keeps him better balanced. This is one
reason the rider should always use his legs in indicating leads; if the

rider merely uses the reins to change direction at the canter, the horse will usually change leads in front but not behind.

A large figure eight is one of the easiest movements in which to teach the flying change of leads. Canter the horse in a large circle on the proper lead, then give him the signal for the other lead as you change directions and begin making the other loop of the "eight." If he has learned his lessons well up to date, he will probably respond by changing leads. It is best to make a large figure eight at first. If it is too small and cramped the horse may fall down if he doesn't change leads, or may merely change leads in front and be disunited.

If the horse refuses to change leads on the figure eight, make a large circle, keeping him in the wrong lead, and gradually cut it smaller and smaller until you can see that it is awkward for the horse to keep cantering on the wrong lead. Then give him the signal to change and he will usually change to the correct lead at once.

Perhaps a better way to teach a horse the flying change is to work to it from a trot. If you are circling to the left at a canter and want to change direction to the right, slow him down to a trot for a few strides, then put him into a canter in the right lead as you change directions. If you always make him change leads (even if you have to slow to the trot temporarily to do it) when you change directions he will learn that when he changes directions he must change leads. You can use a large figure eight, dropping to the trot as you make the change. The horse will more readily take the proper lead when you resume the canter because you have already taught him to take specific leads from the trot, and a few trotting strides will give him time to get his legs ready to go into the new lead. The more you practice, the fewer trotting strides you'll need, and before long you should be able to just check the horse for an instant with the reins and then give the signal for the change of leads. The horse should then make the change in midair.

Try to avoid prolonging any lesson. Flying changes are tiring to the horse, and if he gets tired he may refuse to cooperate. And if he is worked to the point of tiring his reflexes won't be as good and he may stumble or strike a front leg with a hind foot.

As you and the horse become more accustomed to the flying change, you will not need emphatic signals; a slight touch of your leg and the rein will make him change leads for you. When a horse is trained to this point he should be able to change leads at your signal whether he is making a turn or cantering in a straight line. After he is this far along on his training he will be more useful as a stock horse and more ready for fast reining of any kind.

One of the main purposes of training a horse is to have him always in control so that the two of you are working together rather than in opposition. You can't begin to do a good job of riding, whether for pleasure, for work, or for show, until your horse is always where you want him, balanced and with his feet under him properly—until you and your horse work as a unit. And this can only be accomplished after you, his rider, have control of his cantering and his leads.

17

WINTER CARE AND RIDING

The first chapters in this book covered some important aspects of caring for a horse. The last few chapters have dealt with some of the fundamentals of training a horse. Now let's look at some aspects of good riding that tie in with proper care of the horse. The first subject we'll cover is riding and caring for the horse in wintertime. In the next chapter we'll look at proper conditioning of the horse for riding after any layoff.

Whatever the climate is in your part of the country, here in the northwest we have cold winters and snow. Even though our eastern Idaho winters might be different from where you live, perhaps some of our ideas and suggestions may be helpful to you, too.

Lynn and I consider ourselves fortunate in the location of our ranch. The winters in our valley are usually mild compared to those of the surrounding areas. Montana, except the mountainous western part which is similar to our country, often has severe winters for livestock. Some of southern Idaho has the same problem because of the flatness of the land. In these windy places livestock must have winter shelter because wind makes the "temperature" much colder than the thermometer states, creating an actual survival problem if the temperature drops very low. A rough rule of thumb to give you some idea of the difference made by the wind: each mile per hour of wind is approximately equal to a degree lower in temperature. You can see why so many livestock in the West froze to death several winters ago in areas where the temperature went down to forty below zero, accompanied by fifty- and sixty-mile-an-hour winds—the equivalent of ninety or a hundred below zero on a still day!

But here in our valley we are protected by the surrounding mountains and we don't often have strong winds. Temperatures sometimes get down into the thirties below zero, but when it is that cold here the air is still; there is no devastating wind to penetrate winter hair and whip away all body heat. Our horses do not seem to suffer from the cold. The weather that bothers them most comes generally in the fall or spring or during a freak warm-weather winter storm—when they get soaked with rain or melting snow and then chilled by lowering temperatures before they have dried off. These are the times they seem most susceptible to colds. Yet when kept in good condition a horse will rarely catch cold.

In caring for our horses in winter, several items are of great importance. First, we are concerned with the condition of our horses as winter begins. A thin horse will not winter as well as a fat one. Horses should never be *too* fat, but they should be carrying enough extra flesh at the beginning of winter to remain healthy and to have some reserve for extra energy and body heat, since most of our horses winter "out" on winter range or pasture and generally get no extra feeding except under severe weather conditions. Even if fed well all winter, a horse going into the winter thin will not do as well as one that is carrying enough flesh, for the thin one has no reserves. It is a lot easier to get a horse into good condition before winter starts than after the cold weather sets in.

Old horses and young horses winter harder than mature horses in their prime. An old horse, because of poor teeth or a combination of other factors (perhaps including lower resistance to cold and less ability to "bounce back" rapidly after storms or other circumstances which drain away reserves of body heat and energy) needs to go into the winter carrying a good deal of extra flesh. The condition of an old horse when going into the winter season may well determine whether he will survive for just one or a few more seasons or many. If he goes downhill too badly during the winter it will take him a long time to get back into good condition the next summer. For some old horses, one bad winter is enough to tip the scales; it's too great a strain on them and they never seem quite the same afterward, continually drifting downhill. Unless he is fat and a "good keeper," we don't let an old horse winter out, but keep him at the ranch and feed him extra.

Mature horses on winter pasture do not need grain if they have good pasture or hay. But young horses—weanlings, yearlings, and two-year-olds—do much better if fed grain. They are less apt to be stunted or set back in their growth if fed liberally during the winter. Remember that these young horses need sufficient nutrition for *growth* as well as for energy and body heat during cold weather. I have seen "weedy," stunted, poorly developed two- and three-year-olds—horses that wintered out on pasture that was good enough for mature horses but insufficient for growing ones. We like our dry-land range pastures for our young stock—

the dry-land grasses are good horse feed and the steep terrain is ideal for developing balance, dexterity, surefootedness, good muscle, and wind —but unless we are able to feed them supplementary grain daily, we keep our young horses close at hand at the ranch where we can feed them adequately.

Another factor to be considered in caring for horses during winter is shelter. The horse is a rugged animal, one of the most adaptable creatures in the animal kingdom, as you can tell when you consider the many different climates around the world in which he seems to thrive. Most horses in our part of the country winter out; they never see a barn, and they seem none the worse for it. But this doesn't mean they don't have shelter. Shelter *is* important. Our ranch and our ranges have canyons and draws, places where horses and cattle can get out of the wind. And the brushy areas in these draws and along the creek bottom provide a great deal of shelter, not only as windbreaks, but also give some relief from driving snow or rain. In pastures where there are no "natural" wind-breaks or shelter of any sort, a simple three-sided open shed will provide adequate shelter. Horses seem to prefer being out of doors even in the coldest and most inclement weather, but they do appreciate a good windbreak.

A good general rule to follow concerning shelter during storms and cold weather is that it's usually best for a horse to stay in an environment that he is accustomed to. If you keep your horse in the barn every night and he is used to it, by all means put him in the barn during stormy and cold weather. But if he is accustomed to being outdoors, do *not* bring him into the barn just because of foul weather. If he is accustomed to a blanket, keep it on him and keep it dry. But if he is not used to a blanket, leave it off. Bringing a horse into the barn and blanketing him when he is not used to it may actually bring on a bad cold; he may become overheated and sweat and then become chilled.

Some horsemen try to care for their horses too well, especially when the weather threatens to be bad. As mentioned before, a horse in good condition is best left to fend for himself. Horses were meant to be out-side; it is their natural environment. It's not necessary to cover them or bring them inside, so long as they have a chance to toughen them-selves naturally and gradually as the winter comes on. They grow thick hair as part of their protection from wind and cold. If you keep a horse blanketed in order to prevent this extra hair growth—to keep him in "show shape"—he will not grow a winter coat and obviously can't be expected to stand out in a winter storm. It's not wise to clip and blanket a horse in preparation for shows if the horse will have to spend some of his time outside exposed to winter weather.

Nor is it wise to take a horse from one climate to another without the necessary precautions. We know some folks from southern California who came to Idaho one fall to go elk hunting. They brought along a horse to ride and to pack out their meat. But the horse was used to a warm climate and had no protective winter coat. Our fall weather was wet and cold that year and this horse became thoroughly chilled, came down with a bad case of pneumonia, and they nearly lost him.

When traveling in winter with your horse from one climate to another you must take the necessary steps to keep him comfortable and healthy. But traveling in cold climates will not bother a horse that is accustomed to cold weather. We have trailered our horses in cold and snowy weather for hunting trips without blanketing them or enclosing them and they seem to take it in stride. This is because they are used to the cold and are "dressed" for it naturally.

Nature usually takes care of her children very well and we can learn a lot from her. But sometimes a horseman's circumstances or situation prevents him from letting his horses live in a "natural" environment. If you do keep your horse inside, keep him dry. If he is blanketed, don't let his blanket get wet from rain or melting snow, or from his own sweat. Even in cold weather a horse can become too warm under a blanket and start sweating, and this moisture under the blanket does not evaporate as will the moisture on an uncovered horse. The blanketed horse may chill and become susceptible to a cold or pneumonia.

If ever you must bring a wet horse indoors because of sickness or injury or some other problem, make sure you get him thoroughly dry. Rub him with cloths or sacks until you have gotten all the moisture you can, then groom him with vigorous brushing. Rubbing and brushing help dry him not only by getting rid of excess moisture, but also by stimulating his circulation, making him warmer.

Never expose the horse to drafts. Drafts can cause chilling and colds, especially if the horse is damp. The horse is better off outside in the open than inside a drafty place. The cold will not bother him outside, but a light, gusty little bit of air moving around his stall or through the barn can bring on a bad cold.

If your horse is kept outside, as ours are, he should have some sort of shelter, as mentioned earlier. He should have water. Horses drink less water in cold weather, but they still need it. Horses will eat snow, and they will do better than cattle on snow alone, but they still need some water to get sufficient moisture for bodily functions.

Our horses range on 320 acres of dry-land pasture with a spring at the top end and a little creek running the length of one side. They seem to like the high ridges best—grass is tall and the wind blows the snow away so they can easily get at it. In very cold weather the spring freezes

Lynn on Bambi—checking cattle on a winter day.

up and the creek freezes solid except in one or two places. Still the horses prefer to stay on the ridges and eat snow, only coming down to the creek every few days for a big drink of water, even though they travel widely daily.

We rarely feed hay on this winter pasture, for grass is usually available on the ridges or the south slopes and the horses don't have to do much pawing to get at it. The south slopes receive more winter sun and often melt off several times during the winter, whereas the north slopes stay shaded and the snow piles up deeper and deeper. After an unusually heavy snowfall we take hay in the jeep up to the horses. Even in deep snow they will paw through to grass, but they need strength to do it, so we feed them right after a heavy snowfall. Then when it begins to melt off and the wind begins to peel the snow from the ridges the horses will have energy to go out and graze and paw through to grass. Generally, in a few days the snow is once again swept from the ridges and melted from some of the south slopes.

Do not overfeed a horse during a severe storm. He needs his blood circulating to keep him warm and not tied up in the digestive process. If most of his blood is concentrated around his digestive tract, he may chill. Wait until after the storm is over to feed him extra.

One warning when feeding hay in winter—hay that is freshly wet from a storm is all right to feed, but hay that has been wet for more

than a few hours (especially alfalfa hay) can begin to mold. And pellets
can be dangerous when damp. Usually there is no danger in feeding hay
or pellets to horses on winter pasture. They are glad of the change from
dry grass and clean up the feed quickly. But if you feed too much and
the damp hay or pellets are not cleaned up right away they can cause
digestive upsets when eaten later.

If a horse is to be on winter pasture, his shoes should be removed
so that his feet can grow and have a chance to wear normally. Also, there
will be no chance of a shoe catching in a wire fence and entangling the
horse, and snow will not ball up under his feet to make slippery footing.
A barefoot horse can get around a little better on ice and snow than a
horse with ordinary shoes. On sheer ice a horse gets around best if
he is shod with special "sharp" shoes, but in snow he is better off barefoot.
There are some situations in which it is best to leave a horse's shoes on,
for example, an extremely rocky pasture with very little snow cover.
Another circumstance would be a horse wintering where there is such
deep snow that he must paw through the snow for all his grass. Some
ranchers whose horses winter out in deep snow leave front shoes on
their horses so they won't wear their feet down to the quick pawing
continually for food. But if a horse wears shoes all winter the shoes
must be removed and reset periodically after trimming the feet, or the

Warm clothing for winter riding. My father, on Khamette, wearing chaps;
Lynn, on Bambi, wearing coveralls.

Checking through the cattle.

horse's feet will grow too long and put strain on bones and tendons or even cripple the horse if they are left too long.

Riding in winter can be a pleasure if a person is dressed properly but very unpleasant if he is not. Warm clothing is a must, but warm lightweight clothing is better than bulky wear. If you are too heavily bundled you cannot move freely. This can pose a problem when working cattle or when trying to mount and dismount. Proper clothing should keep you warm and dry, and not be too burdensome. Wool is a good material for insulation against the cold; it can absorb a lot of moisture (sweat) and still keep the air next to your skin dry. Clean wool clothing worn loosely is good insulation against cold and has enough ventilation to evaporate accumulated moisture. An outer jacket containing down, wool, fur, or synthetic fiber gives an insulated layer of warm air.

On windy days you'll want a scarf or knitted face mask to protect your nose and cheeks from frostbite. The danger of frostbite is much greater when the wind is blowing, for as we stated in the beginning of this chapter, wind makes the temperature much colder than the thermometer registers. You might expect danger of frostbite at twenty below zero and be prepared for it, but you're just as likely to suffer frostbite at a much warmer temperature if there is some wind. And don't forget that when you and your horse are moving, it will have the same effect on your exposed skin as if a wind were blowing. If you and your horse are traveling ten miles per hour on a still day, exposed skin is subjected to a ten-miles-per-hour wind.

Your feet will tend to get cold when you are riding unless you have warm footwear. This means some kind of boot roomy enough for a warm sock or even two pairs of socks. A boot that is too tight will make your feet cold even if you have warm socks on, because a tight boot shuts off circulation. Circulation is very important. I've discovered that those of us who "ride with our legs" and feet generally have warmer feet than the person who merely sits on his horse as a passenger, never moving his legs. A good rider uses his stirrups, and uses his legs in communicating with the horse, whether he's asking for a turn, urging a fast walk, or just keeping the horse collected. It's amazing how much difference this can make, both in the response of the horse and in keeping your feet warm!

Lynn and I sometimes wear chaps in extremely cold or wet weather to keep our legs warm and dry. Chaps are wonderful when we have to ride through woods or brushy areas, protecting our legs and keeping them from getting soaked when snow and water clinging to the bushes brushes off onto our legs.

I've mentioned the rider's comfort. Now let's look at the comfort of the horse. A horse being ridden steadily during the winter should be fed well, receiving grain as well as hay or pasture. On cold days when you ride, warm the bit in your hand before you put it in his mouth. An icy-cold bit on a warm tongue is cruel, especially if it is so cold that his tongue freezes to it for an instant before his body heat warms it up. Brush any snow or moisture from his back before you saddle him.

In riding, use caution and good judgment in slippery places or deep snow. In deep snow or in drifts your horse may become unsure of himself or panicky and plunge through it, wearing himself out. Avoid deep drifts, and keep him well-collected when he is unsure of himself. But this does not mean rigid restraint; he may need the use of his head and neck for balance if he is on unsure footing.

Remember that snow can pack and ball up badly in a shod hoof. A wet, packing snow under a shod horse will soon have him walking on four balls of ice—very slippery indeed. Under these conditions it is good to grease the bottom of his feet with a substance such as oil or warm vaseline (cold vaseline won't stick to his foot) which will keep the snow from sticking.

Packed snow is more slippery than undisturbed snow. Beware of packed roadways and trails, especially when going downhill. Horses seem more apt to slip and slide going downhill than on the level or going uphill. But steep uphill travel on slick surfaces can be very dangerous, too.

Riding from lower ranch to the upper ranch in winter.

If the going is slippery, walk. If you must go faster, as we sometimes need to when herding or sorting cattle, even a trot is always safer than a gallop. A horse has much more control on slick or steep or uneven ground at the trot than at a canter or gallop, especially when going downhill. Beware of frozen ground even if there is no snow. Frozen ground can be very slippery—there's not much traction—and a fall on frozen ground is not very pleasant.

One of the most important things to consider in winter riding is to make sure your horse is always cooled out and dry after you ride. In winter the horse has a heavy coat, and if he sweats and becomes damp it will take longer for his normal body heat at rest to dry himself than in summer. His winter skin and hair are good insulation, letting very little body heat escape. Also, the air is cold and it takes longer for this moisture to evaporate. Thus he is wet for a longer period of time than in summer and is doubly susceptible to chilling because of cold weather. If you ride in winter and your horse is hot and sweaty when you finish, take time to cool him properly and dry him. He has done his part in giving you a good ride. Now it's up to you to do your part in caring for him properly to keep him comfortable and healthy.

All too often a horse is unsaddled after a ride and given a rubdown or some brushing for five or ten minutes and is then turned loose in his stall or pasture. This attention is usually sufficient in summer, but not nearly enough in winter. The horse's blood circulation is active during any brisk exercise, but in winter he has a winter skin and winter coat of hair and the radiation of body heat from the blood through the skin is less in winter than in summer. So it takes a longer time to cool a horse in winter.

You can help cool him by giving him mild exercise such as walking, or by massaging his chest and legs and giving him a good rubdown. If he is still breathing rapidly or shallowly or his pulse rate is still higher than usual, he is not yet cool. When at rest, the horse's respiration is about sixteen to twenty breaths a minute, and his pulse rate is about forty. During strenuous exercise his pulse rate and respiration can both get as high as a hundred per minute. After exercise these rates begin to return to normal, and he is not cool until they do.

Sweating is a condition that must be dealt with in winter. It is possible for a horse to still be wet after he has cooled off and his circulation and respiration are back to normal. He should never be turned loose wet. He may chill, especially if you finish your ride at the end of the day and the lower temperatures of night are approaching.

There are two things I want to mention about sweating. First, a horse in good working condition is less apt to sweat a great deal than a soft, unconditioned horse. You can hurt a horse by riding him too hard when he is not conditioned for it, especially in winter when the added factor of being wet and then chilling adds an extra shock to his system. Secondly, what you feed the horse can also make a difference in how much he sweats. We've found that when we feed our horses a large portion of alfalfa hay along with their grass hay or pasture (especially second or third cutting alfalfa that is nearly straight alfalfa) they sweat a great deal more than on a diet of grass hay or pasture, regardless of their conditioning. Lynn and I don't feed the horses much alfalfa hay if we are using them a lot in the winter, for it makes them sweat so much more than usual when they are exercised; then it takes longer to get them dry. It takes a lot of time and work to dry a wet horse, but you dare not just turn him loose wet with a cold night coming on— that's a sure way to invite a bad cold or pneumonia.

As winter moves on into spring we get sudden changes in the weather. There are warm days, and then colder ones again, and some rain now instead of snow. Spring is a hard time for horses. They seem more susceptible to colds—eyes and nose may run, and sometimes they cough. They are shedding their winter coats, but there are still some cold and wet days before spring really arrives. Horses on winter pasture may get thinner at the first signs of spring. They prefer the new green grass to the dry grass or hay, even though there is not yet enough new green grass to give them all the food they need. Supplemental feeding (grain or pellets) can help combat this problem and should be given if spring is slow in coming.

Spring is the time when most of the elk and deer that "winterkill" starve to death. They have survived the tough winter but are now so eager for the green shoots that these are all they will eat, even if there is still some dry feed left. If spring is slow in arriving, the few green spears they find are not nearly enough to support them and they starve.

Horses are a little bit the same. So when winter seems about over and spring is on its way, don't neglect your horses—this may be the time of year they need good care the most.

18

CONDITIONING THE HORSE

Horses should be properly conditioned for their work.

Since most of our horses here on the ranch are kept on winter pasture, except the one or two that we use during the winter, they are out of shape and need to be brought back gradually to working condition before we start our regular summer's work of moving cattle and riding range.

When a horse has been on winter pasture, or at times when he has not been ridden regularly, his muscles are soft. If he is overexercised, he will become stiff and sore. He will also be short of wind. It is never good to overwork a horse when he is out of condition. This can cause strains, sprains, or bruises which a horse in good working condition would not get. Working a horse that is out of condition will tire him, and working a tired horse can result in accidents (such as bad falls, strained tendons, etc.) or in diseases (because of the tired horse's lower resistance).

Some horses on winter pasture become thin toward spring. Others are fat and mushy from lack of regular exercise. All horses that have not been ridden regularly are out of condition. Muscles and tendons are weakened and tight; heart and lungs are not accustomed to exertion.

So, in the spring we need to start feeding our horses properly for the work they will be doing, and "leg them up," gradually strengthening their legs and getting them in condition for summer's riding. Conditioning is building the horse up to the job he will be doing. His speed, stamina, and endurance all depend on the condition he is in—whether his muscles are soft from nonuse or "hard" and fit. A horse must be trained not only to do a specific job (whether it be in the show ring, on the race track, cutting cattle or riding range); he must also have his muscles built up to where he can perform his job with ease and without strain.

Horses by nature are travelers, but they must be conditioned to various distances and terrains. Though we might have ridden our horses as much as thirty or forty miles or more in a day last fall, we can't expect them to go that far when we ride them for the first time this spring. They have to be conditioned back to these distances.

Our first aim in conditioning our horses is to get them in good flesh without excess fat, and gradually increase their work to change the soft fat to hard muscle. We bring the horses down from their winter pasture and put them on regular daily rations—hay and grain if the green grass is not yet adequate. If a horse is thin, he should be fed more than one that is carrying enough flesh, but the increase in feed should take place gradually or he will have stomach disorders, or might even founder.

A word should be mentioned here about new spring grass. I touched on this briefly in the chapter on miscellaneous health problems that included founder, but it won't hurt to mention it again. A horse that has been on hay all winter should not be turned into a green pasture suddenly or he may get "grass founder." In the spring of the year, nature produces a special juice in all plants which stimulates new growth, causing them to bud and blossom. This same juice is in new green grass and can cause a horse to founder if he eats too much of it all at once. Horses that have been on dry winter feed should get used to new spring pasture very slowly—perhaps twenty or thirty minutes the first day, an hour the second, several hours the third, and then full time the fourth day if the horse seems to suffer no ill effects. There is no danger to horses that are kept in a pasture during the transition from winter to spring. They will eat the new green grass as soon as it appears, but there won't be enough at first to hurt them and they will adjust to it naturally as the grass gradually becomes thicker and flourishes.

When you begin riding your horse it might be wise to have him wormed. He can then utilize more of his feed and get in shape faster. And remember that conditioning is not a rapid process. You are trying to build muscle and stamina. If you push the horse too fast, riding him too much too soon, you will be tearing down rather than building up. The horse is an athlete, and like a human athlete, he has to train and build up his muscles gradually. As the horse's work increases, his feed may have to be increased—this, after all, is where his energy comes from.

We keep a close watch on our horses to see whether they gain weight, stay the same or lose weight as we condition them. A conditioned horse is hard, and he won't be carrying as much flesh as a soft horse; his fat has changed to muscle. But there is a difference between a hard horse and an undernourished one. A hard horse may not be

202 YOUR HORSE AND YOU

carrying much extra fat, but he is in "good flesh" and is fit and healthy.

Let's look at a typical day of riding early in the conditioning period, when we begin "legging up" our horses. If we feed grain before we start the ride, we feed only a small amount and feed it at least half an hour or forty-five minutes before we start. It's never good to stuff a horse with hay or grain and then expect him to work on a crammed stomach. If my horse is being fed hay, I feed her early in the morning so she will have finished it and has had time to digest it before I ride. I never like to ride a horse that has recently been eating hay; his stomach is so full that he doesn't feel like working.

Rides should always begin at the walk, even after the horse is in excellent condition. Warm your horse up gradually and let him get his digestive tract "cleaned out" before doing any faster work. Ten or fifteen minutes at the walk will establish good circulation. Many horses do not perform well until they are warmed up.

On the first few rides in the spring, or after any long layoff, we complete the entire ride at the walk, with perhaps an occasional trot on successive rides. To strengthen his legs and build up his wind, the horse needs to go miles and miles at the walk. On each following ride we gradually trot more, and after the horse begins to get in condition,

Rides should always begin at the walk. Here is an old photo of my brother (at the left, on Scrappy), my father on Old Possum, and me on Ginger—leaving the ranch to ride range.

Traveling through some of the low range.

we add an occasional canter to help build up his wind. By the third or fourth week we are trotting and cantering, alternating each gait with the walk.

A change of gaits is restful to the horse as long as the faster gaits are not overdone. Our horses are usually beginning to get in good condition by the time we turn our cattle out on summer range in late May or early June (we've been using them on short regular rides around the ranch, moving cattle from one pasture to another, checking on cows, doctoring calves, and so forth). The range riding we do during the summer, traveling many miles daily at the walk and trot in steep terrain, with an occasional canter or gallop to turn an unruly cow when moving cattle, continues to build up the horses' fitness and wind and they are soon hard and able to travel well all day.

In starting to condition a horse for strenuous riding, notice how he sweats. When he is out of condition his sweat will be white and lathery, appearing first between his hind legs and on his neck. If he sweats profusely the first time you ride him, you may be working him too hard. As he gets in better condition the sweat will be more clear and watery and when he is in good condition he should be able to do a great deal of work without sweating, unless the weather is quite warm.

Clear, watery sweat is nothing to worry about, for it helps cool a horse that is doing strenuous work on a hot day. Horses should always

Climbing a hill on the high range.

have salt available, especially if they are doing hard work, to replace the salt lost through sweating.

At the end of every ride we try to walk our horses the last mile or two home. Then they are cooled and dry and can be unsaddled and turned loose without extra cooling-out procedures. If a horse is galloped home hot and then has to stand panting and sweating, he will cool off too rapidly and his muscles will stiffen. This is never good for a horse. Sometimes we must take extra measures to cool our horses, after coming home through steep hills or bringing cattle home through the hills— a task that can be a lot of hard work for the horses if the cattle are not cooperative. If the horses are still hot when we get home, we walk them and then brush them vigorously.

We are careful about the way we take our saddles off after a long hard ride. After riding many hours there has been quite a bit of pressure on the horse's back and the blood has been somewhat pressed out of the area. If a rider got off suddenly and took his saddle off, this pressure would be released all at once and a lot of blood would rush into the area. This can sometimes cause permanent lumps and bumps on the horse's back. If we've been on a long ride, we sometimes get off and lead the horse part of the last way home, relieving some of the pressure on his back. Or we loosen the cinch a little and leave the horse's saddle on for a while before taking it off, perhaps leading the horse a bit in the meantime, and lifting the saddle a couple times to let blood begin to return to the area. Massaging the horse's back after the saddle is removed can prevent "heat bumps" and can also help to remove them if they do form.

It is good to groom a horse after every ride. If he is still warm, brushing will help cool him properly. It stimulates circulation and will keep him from getting chilled after strenuous exercise.

Muscle fatigue, due to accumulation of waste products in the muscle cells, occurs after a horse has worked long and strenuously (an unconditioned horse fatigues sooner and more easily because his muscles carry an excess of fat). As soon as the accumulated waste products are carried away by the blood, the horse begins to feel fresh and fit again. Grooming, massaging, and rubbing of the horse's legs after strenuous exercise stimulates circulation and helps in the removal of waste products; grooming and massaging the horse can help combat excessive tiredness. A horse that is not cooled out thoroughly or properly will sometimes break out in a second sweat.

After our horses are cooled, we water them sparingly if they are thirsty, but we don't let them drink their fill until we have unsaddled and groomed them. By that time they are usually cool enough to be turned loose to eat or drink as they choose. Never let a horse have much water when he is hot. It cools him much too rapidly and can cause founder, as explained in an earlier chapter. When we are riding range or moving cattle and our horses have been working hard, we let them have ten or twelve swallows of water when we come to a stream or a spring, but we don't let them "tank up." A few swallows refresh the horse and partially satisfy his thirst.

A point that should be mentioned about conditioning: it is possible to *over*condition a horse, and this is not good.

By the time our ranch horses are in good condition they are able to travel great distances, as much as fifty miles or more in a day's work. They are able to withstand the rigors of a strenuous day checking cattle, or moving or sorting cattle, often having to trot and canter up and down very steep terrain. But we do not require this sort of effort from them *every* day. This is one reason we have several horses on our ranch. If one horse had to do all the work that the horses one of us ride do during the summer, it would soon wear out. It is possible to "burn out" a horse, even a good horse that has a great deal of stamina. When we make a long or strenuous ride two or three days in a row, we use fresh horses. Even riders who condition their horses for endurance rides do not go great distances every day. They ride twenty to forty miles perhaps two or three times a week, with shorter rides or days of rest spaced in between.

On days of rest we do not feed our horses as much as on the days they work. A horse doing strenuous work and getting a good ration of grain should have the ration cut down considerably on days he does not work to avoid digestive and muscular complications such as azoturia.

When we are conditioning our horses, and when we work them strenuously during the summer, we often make use of a little knowledge of pulse rate and respiration rate. The average normal horse at rest breathes about eight to twenty-four times a minute (sixteen times per minute is average). When walking, his respiration rate nearly triples, and goes even higher when he trots, canters, climbs a steep hill, or does other strenuous work. But if he is in good condition, his respiration slows back down to normal within a short while after stopping.

The pulse rate in a normal horse at rest is thirty-six to fifty beats per minute, forty to forty-four beats being average. When doing strenuous exercise the pulse rate may climb to 120 or even higher. The heartbeat of a conditioned horse will return to normal (usually within an hour) sooner after exertion than that of an unconditioned horse.

The heartbeat and breathing rate of an unconditioned horse increases rapidly when he starts to exercise, whereas the pulse and respiration of a conditioned horse rises at first and then tapers off, rising only gradually until finally the pulse and respiration are as rapid as those of the unconditioned horse. In other words, the soft horse may be panting and his heart pounding after climbing one steep hill at the beginning of the ride. The hard horse may go several hours and many miles, up many hills, before his heartbeat and breathing become this rapid.

In any horse, when the respiration rate becomes faster than the pulse rate—when the horse is panting and breathing very rapidly and shallowly—he has reached a point of exhaustion in which his overall condition is endangered. To push a horse beyond this point is impractical. You are tearing him down instead of building him up. When conditioning a horse it is never good to push him past this point. We have much steep terrain on our range, and if a horse's breathing becomes too rapid, we let him stop and rest. An unconditioned horse may need to stop two or three times or even oftener when going up a very steep slope. A conditioned horse will not need to stop nearly so often, but we stop him for a breather whenever his respiration does become rapid. A conditioned horse will be able to go much farther in a day if he is allowed to rest when he needs to.

A soft horse should be allowed to rest frequently so that he can regain his breath. The ride should end before he becomes too fatigued. When a horse is extremely fatigued, he has a very high pulse and respiration rate, with respiration clearly going higher than the pulse. If he is pushed past this point very far his temperature, which up until now has been slightly above normal due to exertion, will drop suddenly into subnormal

Pausing at the top of a hill to rest the horses. Rockwell and Khamette, Heidi and Nosey, and Nell's ears.

ranges and he will be in a state of shock. A horse should never be ridden to this point; not only his health but his life is in danger.

A conditioned horse can put in a hard day's work and be saved from extreme fatigue by wise and careful riding and a few strategic rest stops. Knowing when a horse is reaching the point of fatigue is very useful to anyone who depends on his horse to carry him strongly and freshly all day.

We can usually feel when a horse is reaching the point where he needs a rest without actually counting heartbeats and breathing rate, but it is sometimes interesting to take a count just for accuracy's sake and to see how close the pulse and respiration really are.

It is a little easier to get a pulse and respiration count from the ground, so sometimes when we stop the horse to rest we dismount and get a count. When the horse has been exercising strenuously you can get a count on his breathing rate just by sight and sound (although when the horse first stops to rest it is hard to get an accurate count because his breathing begins slowing down immediately). His breathing may be audible. Or you can watch his nostrils or his flanks, or feel his breath on your cheek. You can listen to his respiration in the windpipe with your ear pressed against the horse's neck, or you can feel the movement of his flanks. This last way is a good way to get a respiration count when you are mounted and traveling; you can usually reach far enough down from the saddle to feel the flank movements.

The pulse can be taken at several sites: under the jawbone at the lower part of the flat muscle near the cheek side, on the horse's pastern just above the bulb of the heels, along the horse's neck, and in his chest (listening to heartbeat). But for all practical purposes when we are riding range or conditioning a horse, we can "feel" when the horse needs to rest. It isn't difficult to sense when the horse is breathing hard, and a little knowledge and understanding of the individual horse and his way of traveling helps us tell when he should stop to rest.

Some horses stop on their own when they approach this point, and to push them on is foolhardy. Bambi is this way. Others are more eager travelers and will "go until they drop." These horses must be stopped to rest or they will hurt themselves. We have several horses that would go too far if the rider does not stop them to rest; they are eager travelers and a joy to ride. But just because a horse keeps going doesn't mean that he doesn't need rest.

Horses are usually willing animals, and as a general rule will wear themselves out if the rider lets them. A mule will stop when he needs to (even if his rider or driver urges him on, he will usually be stubborn and want to stop). A mule won't push himself too far. But a horse will sometimes keep going even when he is hurting himself, especially if the rider keeps urging him on. We call this "heart," and appreciate it in a good horse, but it is up to us as horsemen to use good judgment when we ride, not urging a horse past his abilities nor letting a willing one keep going when he shouldn't.

Some horses are lazy and stop before they need to. These horses can be pushed on until they really do need a rest. The first horse I ever owned, Old Possum, was that sort. My father bought him for me when I was nine. Possum was a great old gelding in his twenties and served us faithfully for many years; he finally died at the age of thirty-two. He was a smart old fellow and took as good care of himself as any mule, never overdoing, never straining himself, conservative in his movements, always saving energy. He would take advantage of an inexperienced rider, feigning tiredness or lameness. A person unaccustomed to his ways could not get much work out of him. But he could put forth a good day's work on the range and travel as many miles as our younger horses if you knew him. Even when he worked cattle or traveled all day in the hills, he never overworked himself. I never saw him sweat but once in all the times we rode him.

We've talked about the condition of the horse. Perhaps a word should be added about the conditioning of the rider. A rider as well as his horse needs to be "hard" if he wants to be able to ride all day or be able to aid his horse's performance. A tired rider makes a tired horse. When a rider

Resting the horses and enjoying the peaceful beauty of the high range.

gets tired he sags and slouches; he is not "with" his horse and creates a drag on the horse, adding extra pounds and strain because he is not always in balance with the horse. A rider who sags or slouches in the saddle, riding sloppily, can hurt the horse's kidneys or give the horse a sore back.

When we ride range all day we try to ride as best we can—to help the horse instead of hinder him. We need his ability to do his best and still come home with reserve energy in case we find a situation on the way home that needs our attention—perhaps a cow in the hayfield, some cattle down on the road that need to be moved back up into the hills, maybe a sick cow that needs to be cut out and brought home to doctor. And we may need the horse to be able to carry us again strongly all day tomorrow or the next day if need be. We don't want him excessively fatigued, stiff or sore in any way from sloppy riding on our part.

We ride as balanced as we can, "with" the horse, keeping our weight forward where the horse can handle it with least effort, especially going up (and down!) steep hills. The horse does his part by carrying us strongly and willingly for many long hours and miles.

We should be able to do ours!

IN CLOSING. . . .

This book has touched on a wide variety of subjects, some in detail, others more briefly in passing. But through it all I hope it conveys some basic essentials of good horsemanship. This, in the final analysis, is my aim: to try to promote better understanding, better communication between horse and horseman—through a wider knowledge of the horse, his abilities, his attitudes, his ailments—and therefore help foster good care of the horse, and good horsemanship.

Working with horses can be satisfying, frustrating, challenging, rewarding. And it should be all of these. The good horseman is one who is ever spurred on to wider understanding, whether it be through success or failure; he constantly learns through experience. And don't forget that no matter how much you learn through reading, this book included, experience is the best teacher. Good luck, and best wishes!

INDEX